1984

THE MODERN POETS SERIES   William

S0-BOL-401

3 0301 00086677 8

THE ACHIEVEMENT OF JAMES DICKEY

A COMPREHENSIVE SELECTION OF HIS POEMS WITH A CRITICAL INTRODUCTION

LAURENCE LIEBERMAN
University of Illinois

SCOTT, FORESMAN AND COMPANY

LIBRARY
College of St. Francis
JOLIET, ILL.

Library of Congress Catalog Card No. 68-22742
Copyright © 1968 by Scott, Foresman and Company, Glenview, Illinois 60025
All Rights Reserved. Printed in the United States of America.
Regional offices of Scott, Foresman and Company are located in Atlanta,
Dallas, Glenview, Palo Alto, and Oakland, N. J.

Photograph of James Dickey on front cover by Christopher Dickey.

Pen and ink drawing on back cover by Richard Koppe.

Copyright © 1957, 1961, 1962, 1963, 1964, 1965, 1966, 1967 by James Dickey. "The Hospital Window" and "The Firebombing" appeared originally in Poetry; "The Lifeguard," "The Heaven of
Animals," "In the Tree House at Night," "The Dusk of Horses," "Springer Mountain," "Cherrylog
Road," "In the Marble Quarry," "The Ice Skin," "Bums, on Waking," "The Shark's Parlor," "Sun,"
"Power and Light," "Encounter in the Cage Country," "False Youth: Two Seasons II," and "Falling"
appeared originally in The New Yorker. From Poems 1957-1967 by James Dickey; reprinted by per-
mission of Wesleyan University Press.

811.5
D553l

for **MY MOTHER AND FATHER**

108,776

Other Books in The Modern Poets Series are:
THE ACHIEVEMENT OF THEODORE ROETHKE
THE ACHIEVEMENT OF ROBERT LOWELL
THE ACHIEVEMENT OF BROTHER ANTONINUS
THE ACHIEVEMENT OF RICHARD EBERHART

Books by James Dickey

INTO THE STONE. New York, Charles Scribner's Sons, 1960.
DROWNING WITH OTHERS. Middletown, Wesleyan University Press, 1962.
HELMETS. Middletown, Wesleyan University Press, 1964.
THE SUSPECT IN POETRY. Madison, Minn., The Sixties Press, 1964.
BUCKDANCER'S CHOICE. Middletown, Wesleyan University Press, 1965.
POEMS: 1957-1967. Middletown, Wesleyan University Press, 1967.

CONTENTS

JAMES DICKEY (1923-   )

Since the publication in 1960 of his first volume of poetry, *Into the Stone*, James Dickey's career in poetry has developed with remarkable rapidity. Four volumes, the last a nearly comprehensive collection of poems written in the decade 1957-1967, have followed the first.

James Dickey was born in Atlanta and attended Clemson College, where he excelled at football, and Vanderbilt University, from which he graduated Phi Beta Kappa. He served in the Air Force during both World War II and the Korean War, flying nearly a hundred combat missions and winning three decorations for bravery. Following a year in France on a fellowship from the *Sewanee Review*, he spent six years (1955-1961) with advertising agencies in New York and Atlanta. He abandoned a successful business career in 1961 to spend a year abroad on a Guggenheim fellowship with his wife Maxine and two sons. Since then, Dickey has been poet-in-residence at Reed College (1963-1964) and at San Fernando Valley State College (1964-1965).

An enthusiastic outdoorsman and hunter, Dickey is also a virtuoso on the guitar, able to perform successful imitations of many well-known stylists. His ability to "perform" his poetry for audiences has made him one of the most popular readers on the college circuit, and he is well known as a reviewer and critic of poetry.

In 1966 he won the National Book Award in Poetry for his fourth volume of poems, *Buckdancer's Choice*, and in the same year he began a two-year appointment as Poetry Consultant to the Library of Congress.

JAMES DICKEY—THE DEEPENING OF BEING

The poetic vision in James Dickey's fifth volume of poems, *Falling*, contains so much joy that it is incapable of self-pity or self-defeat. There is a profound inwardness in the poems, the inner self always celebrating its strange joy in solitude, or pouring outward, overflowing into the world. No matter how much suffering the poet envisions, the sensibility that informs and animates him is joy in the sheer pleasure of being.

The condition of joy works remarkable transformations, in literature as in life, often converting the tragic condition into a saving buoyancy. This power to transform is typical of the best poems in the romantic tradition. It derives from a special conjunction of the intelligence with the poetic imagination. The transforming joy in Yeats' poetry works its way into the antithetical spheres of private and public life. One measure of the greatness of Yeats' achievement is the expansion in the scope of his vision to include, with equal rigor and authority, personal disasters of the self and global catastrophes such as the Irish Revolution and World War I. The joyful vision of Theodore Roethke, the American poet for whom Dickey feels the strongest spiritual affinity, rarely extends into the political arena; instead, it journeys forever inward, probing darker and more perilous recesses of the interior self. The more tragic emotion —suffering, bitterness, despair—art can absorb and transmute into joyousness of being, the healthier it is. Dickey's vision aspires, above all, to that kind of supernal healthiness, but it moves uneasily into larger sociopolitical issues of War and Race. His joyousness is generous to a fault, uncontrollable—thus working to disadvantage in a few of his most ambitious poems. In "The Firebombing" and "Slave Quarters," for example, the moments of ecstasy threaten to overbalance the moments of agony.

In the four volumes prior to *Falling*, Dickey seems to vacillate, as did Yeats, between two spiritual poles: stoicism and romantic passion. The problem of facing death without fear elicits by turns, now one, now the other, as in "The Ice Skin":

Not knowing whether
I will break before I can feel,

Before I can give up my powers,
Or whether the ice light

1

In my eyes will ever snap off
Before I die.

The ice light, a heroic "masterly shining," is a dispassionate state, a calm radiance of the spirit learned through a series of existential encounters with "the dying" and the "just born." The prevailing spirit of the poem is the power to endure suffering and meet death quietly, with steadiness and poise—a stoical transcendence over death by intellect.

However, Dickey's vision is far more sustaining when he achieves transcendence over death by passion, intensity of self, deepening of being, as in "The Performance," an early war poem that, with "The Jewel," initiates a sequence of war poetry culminating in a poem of the first importance, "The Firebombing."

In making an assessment of Dickey's war poetry we must ask, Does the sum total of the author's writings on the subject of war move us to respond humanely to the massive political crisis of our generation—that is, to respond with the human, or superhuman, compassion and commitment necessary to redress the wrongs, first, in our individual souls, and last, in the soul of our Age?

In "The Performance," the Japanese executioner will have to carry the scars of Donald Armstrong's death in his soul, since, miraculously, Armstrong's ritual performance has converted the mechanical, inhuman relation between executioner and victim into a personal and inescapably spiritual—an existential—encounter:

. . . the headsman broke down
In a blaze of tears, in that light
Of the thin, long human frame
Upside down in its own strange joy,
And, if some other one had not told him,
Would have cut off the feet

Instead of the head . . .

The fatally impersonal relation between man and man is a central dilemma of our time, occurring in its ultimate form in war. In "The Firebombing," Dickey conceives the dilemma of impersonality as being insoluble. The protagonist, however hard he tries, cannot connect spiritually with his victims below. Conversely, in "The Performance," the ritual acrobatic stunts create personal being, restore the I-thou, so that even the headsman, though powerless to disobey his superiors and follow his impulse to spare Armstrong's life, finds a kind of spiritual absolution during the killing. Armstrong's acrobatics transform the killing relation between them into a saving relation, a forgiving relation. Both souls are saved.

If many veterans are content to claim the depersonalization of their acts and the beings from which they sprang—in war time—as grounds for absolving themselves of personal responsibility for their crimes, James Dickey is not. Witness his mercilessly uncompromising self-judgment in "The Jewel." Recalling his years as a fighter pilot, not only does he impute personal involvement to his flying missions, but he remembers feeling the sort of joyful fascination for his life in the cockpit that men ordinarily feel for precious gems. He is a passive lover—mated to his plane—who allows himself to be abducted by the overpowering beauty of the machinery, "being the first to give in/ To the matched priceless glow of the engines." He sees himself lovingly enclosed in the jewel-cockpit, as in the warmth of a womb. Now, years later, in the warmth of the family tent during a holiday, he recalls the pleasure he received from the enclosure of the plane. The old joy floods into the present, mocking his present security, leaving him feeling, once again, more than ever alone in his soul's late night.

"The Jewel" is one of Dickey's earliest attempts to identify and cope with the residue of guilt left by his role in the war. In the poem, the poet sees himself more as a paroled or pardoned criminal than as a survivor. But can he pardon himself? Does he qualify as a spiritual parolee? "The Jewel" is a predecessor of "The Firebombing" in a way the other war poems are not. In "The Performance" and "Drinking from a Helmet," he allows himself to feel the innocence and compassion of the detached bystander, a stance that conveniently removes the persona from his guilt, so the horror of war may be treated as a subject in itself, apart from whatever moral responsibility he may himself feel for perpetrating evil of his own making or perpetuating evil set in motion by the State.

In "Drinking from a Helmet," a new form—employing short self-contained numbered sections in place of the usual stanza units—facilitates a rapid to-and-fro fluctuation between inner experience and external action. It moves almost effortlessly between controlled hallucination and stark realism, a remarkably apt strategy for a poem that sets out to present extraordinary spiritual events in a setting of extreme dehumanization. Written in a tradition of war poetry, running from Wilfred Owen to Randall Jarrell, in which spiritual uplift in the midst of carnage of battle would be unthinkable, Dickey's poem provides uplift as much because of the soul's depravity as in spite of it.

In the opening sections of "Drinking from a Helmet," the level of awareness of the speaker keeps shifting, refocusing. He is possessed by two beings, recognizably separate early in the poem. Who is speaking, I or ultra-I?

> In the middle of combat, a graveyard
> Was advancing after the troops . . .
> A green water-truck stalled out.
> I moved up on it, behind
> The hill that cut off the firing. . . .
>
> I swayed, as if kissed in the brain.

One being perceives everything with a casual directness, a down-to-earthness necessary to mental self-preservation ("A green water-truck stalled out"); the other registers profound ultra-events ("I swayed, as if kissed in the brain"). The two zigzag, at irregular intervals, through the voice of the speaker, without any noticeable jarring of tone. The voice provides a continuum that can contain both irreducible beings, and gradually the two converge and interpenetrate in the vision of the poem's action:

> I threw my old helmet down
> And put the wet one on.
> Warmed water ran over my face.
> My last thought changed, and I knew
> I inherited one of the dead.

The speaker has imbibed and mystically reincarnated the spirit of the dead soldier in his own living spirit by drinking water from the man's helmet.

In the closing sections, as he envisions a plan to transport the dead man's spirit to his brother's home in California, incredible life bursts into the poem:

I would survive and go there,
Stepping off the train in a helmet
That held a man's last thought . . .
I would ride through all
California upon two wheels . . .
Hoping to meet his blond brother,
And to walk with him into the wood
Until we were lost,
Then take off the helmet
And tell him where I had stood,
What poured, what spilled, what swallowed:

And tell him I was the man.

The poem creates the illusion, finally, of being a prayer girding the speaker for a move back into life. The poem is like a launching pad to an actual experience; simultaneously, it contains within itself that future experience and opens into the event-to-be. The barrier between poem and lived act is swept away, just as the threshold between the living and dead soldiers was dissolved earlier in the poem.

In "The Firebombing," also, two beings function simultaneously but separately. In "Helmet," the two beings are coincident in time but move in different psychic levels. In "The Firebombing," present being collides with past being. Both seem to be hopelessly blocked, ineligible for entry into the full import of the experience—one lost in time, the other in moral stupor. Will the collision between the two lost selves, in the dream-dance of flight, result in a clarity of mind within which the unified self may seek absolution through a true confrontation with its crimes? This question comprises the central strategy of "The Firebombing."

At the finish, Dickey explicitly admits his failure to achieve his intended end: to assuage the moral guilt for past crimes by experiencing again the events in the imagination. He tried, through the medium—and medi- ation—of the poem, to feel some of the human horror and shame that his moral conscience tells him he should have felt twenty years before, and thereby to achieve moral expiation through art—the fire in the poem would cleanse the author's soul, purify it, burn away the sense of sin. But he finds, in the most piercingly honest revelation the poem affords, that art itself is an unclean instrument in his hands. The feelings of guilt and horror stirred by the experience of the poem cannot effect catharsis because they are hampered by the remembered sense of beauty and joy felt during the act of murder, "this detachment,/ The honored aesthetic evil,/ The greatest sense of power in one's life."

Early in the poem, it becomes evident to the reader that the moral jeopardy of the present is just as insuperable as that of the past. Self-purification must occur in the world of the suburban present, but the handicap of present prosperity and excess spreads across the poem in a Whitmanesque catalogue of luxuries that quickly accumulate into an insurmountable obstacle to the self's redemption. There are many self-scalding images that take the speaker part way through the complex initiation ceremonies his redemption requires:

It [the blazing napalm] consumes them in a hot
Body-flash, old age or menopause
Of children, clings and burns . . .

If such images don't contain seeds of expiation, how can ideas or slogans, or even direct prayer, redeem him?

Dickey finds himself in much the same position as Claudius, who fails in the sincere attempt to repent of the murder of the elder Hamlet because he still possesses the spoils of the crime, queen and kingdom, and knows he is too weak to give them up. Likewise, not only is Dickey still blessed, or cursed, with the luxuries of the American suburban middle class, but he persists in being as "American as I am, and proud of it." Further, Dickey's incapacity "to get down there or see/ What really happened" can be attributed to other factors. First, the only way you can know exactly what it feels like to see your own child (or your neighbor's) walk through a door "With its ears crackling off/ Like powdery leaves" is to see it actually happen. Second, in writing the poem, Dickey places himself once again in the "blue light" of the "glass treasure-hole," deep in the same "aesthetic contemplation" he felt as he flew over "The *heart* of the fire." His spirit is perplexed by his joy in the act of writing, trapped in the tools of his art.

The poet senses that the experience of the actual firebombing gave birth in his soul to his deepest aesthetic instincts and talents, which he has never before more directly exploited than in the writing of "The Firebombing." Ironically, the poem seems better even for his having interrupted its flow of experience at the finish to comment on its inevitable failure to achieve its main goal:

Absolution? Sentence? No matter;
The thing itself is in that.

Perhaps this is a sort of ironic punishment: the poem gets better as the author backs away from it, refuses to exult over its beauties, insists that the purely human act of salvation from this massive sin is too great a burden for this poem, or indeed any poem, to carry.

How, then, do we account for the success of the poem, not only as art, but as a human (politically human, even) document? How account for the success of a major poem which unconditionally fails to achieve what the author explicitly intended it to achieve? Simply by acknowledging that whatever is not contained in "the thing itself"—the dramatic confrontation between self and its guilt, its crimes, in the action of the poem —cannot be stated parenthetically at the end as an afterthought, a dissipated message. To state it so would be to falsify the poem's central concern and mode of delivery. The writer has attempted the impossible, and he admits it. He is not ready for self-forgiveness yet, because he is not yet able to feel a guilt commensurate with his crimes. Perhaps he never will be ready. These are grave truths, but they are fully realized truths nonetheless, however lacking they may be in the kind of heroism fashionable at peace rallies in the Sixties.

Moreover, if the poem admits its own failure to feel what must be felt, it carries the reader a step closer to having the feelings necessary to spiritual survival, and carries the instrument of language a step closer to meeting the ultimate life-challenge art faces in our time. If we read this poem—and, indeed, all Dickey's best work—with the brain in our eyes, with the intelligence to see what we call a *vision*, we find it to be poetry that constantly sends *us* back from the printed page to the gravest life-challenges.

As a survivor of two wars, Dickey feels spiritually hunted by disinherited beings (pursued by the "downed dead," as in "Pursuit from Under"), who silently accuse him of usurping their birthright to existence, leaving him with intimations of spiritual illegitimacy:

Out of grief, I was myself
Conceived, and brought to life

To replace the incredible child . . .
Dead before I was born.
                        —"The String"

In a number of war poems—"The Firebombing" particularly—Dickey feels like a cosmic criminal who, by luck or trickery, has miraculously escaped punishment and walks in freedom while innocent souls rot in purgatorial confinement, serving an eternal sentence for another's, his, crimes. He finds most harrowing the thought that he has been personally responsible for the death of many Japanese women and children, and in some poems he tries desperately to make his peace with the phantoms from death's dream kingdom.

Another source of these psychic misgivings is the stories he was often told by his parents about the brother who was "dead before I was born," stories antedating his war years by long enough to have been buried deeply in his memory, ready to be disinterred years later. The stories became indelibly, if invisibly, stamped on his impressionable young mind, and they haunted his early childhood, when he often felt as if he were possessed by a disembodied alter-self, living "within another's life." This long-forgotten obsession revisits him in his early poems, and he shapes it into a unique personal myth or legend. It is the first in a chain of mystiques that embody Dickey's developing logos of being.

To assuage his inexplicable guilt, the poet seeks devices for the revival of dead beings. In "The String," the dying brother's string-tricks, such as "foot of a crow," are conceived of as the ritual magic that can guarantee his eternal return in living beings. The performance can be imitated by the living and used as a way of entering the dead child's being or of taking his being into oneself. The ritual performance with the string converted the brother's dying into an act of love. But it was purely self-love. There was no hint of the child's reaching out to others—parents or friends—through the string-game. Contrarily, the speaker's performance with the string is a love act that engages the other being deeply. It connects him with the dead brother, and he aspires to use it to connect the living parents to the brother, but fails: "I believe in my father and mother/ Finding no hope in these lines."

A comparison between "The String" and the later "Power and Light" can be used to illustrate the remarkable distance Dickey's art has traveled between his first book and *Falling*. In "The String" he connects his own being to the Other, the spirits of the dead, but cannot, or will not, mediate between others as a neutral, but fiercely charged, spiritual conductor, as in "Power and Light":

                        and I feel the wires running
Like the life-force along the limed rafters   and all connections
With poles   with the tarred naked belly-buckled black
Trees I hook to my heels   with the shrill phone calls leaping
Long distance   long distances through my hands   all connections

Even the one
With my wife, turn good . . . Never think I don't know my profession
Will lift me: why, all over hell the lights burn in your eyes,
People are calling each other   weeping with a hundred thousand
Volts   making deals   pleading   laughing like fate,
Far off, invulnerable   or with the right word pierced

To the heart
By wires I held, shooting off their ghostly mouths,
In my gloves.

The power lines of this poem exceed the string by the same vast margin as "Power and Light" surpasses "The String" in spiritual intensity.

   In "The String," as in most poems in *Into the Stone*, ritual hangs back from the reader in an ephemeral landscape of dream-memory. The reader is enticed by the strangeness of images, and if he feels somehow left outside the speaker's experience—a charmed, but displaced, on-looker—he is persuaded mentally by the ingenuity of the poem's argu-ment:

My eyes go from me, and down
Through my bound, spread hands
To the dead, from the kin of the dead . . .

In a number of the earlier poems, however, the gap between the reader's life-experience and the poem's drama is too large. In an attempt to bridge the gap, the mind's activity, in the form of willed images or willed ideas, dominates the poem. The reader recoils from the tone of intellectual stridency as the poem's everextended machinery quavers like a house of cards.

In contrast, in many lines of "In the Tree House at Night," a later poem that revives the dead brother's spirit, there *is* something of the lightness of air—one can almost hear inbreathing sounds, a wind-sucking voice:

The floor and walls wave me slowly . . .
In the arm-slender forks of our dwelling

I breathe my live brother's light hair.

It is perhaps no accident that in the early poems we find the inexplicable beginnings of a vision of genesis in air that eventually develops into the fulfilled air-birth of Dickey's most achieved vision, in "Falling." Unlike the play-dwellings of "The String," the hypnotic lyricism of "Tree House" creates a castle in air that takes the reader's heaviness away and converts him into a being afloat, a just-lighter-than-air self. The poem's drama instills the sense of flying, of a soul set free in its body:

When may I fall strangely to earth,

Who am nailed to this branch by a spirit?

In "Tree House," atmospheric elements of scene, setting, time of day— all become dynamically enmeshed in the poem's drama. As in a movie, these elements create the illusion of action taking place *now*. The ritual magic of the poem's movement pulls the reader, irresistibly, into its happening. He is himself one of the actors, sharing the tree house of the poem's ritual flight with "My brothers and I, one dead,/ The other asleep from much living,/ In mid-air huddled beside me."

In "Tree House," as in the other best poems of the second volume, *Drowning with Others*, Dickey evolves a mode of experiencing a double vision that seems ideally suited to his poetic imagination, thereby anticipating the more complex dualism of later poems like "Drinking from a Helmet" and "Firebombing." Two separate, but interdependent, dramas occur simultaneously in "Tree House." A familiar scene or event is presented directly, and an equally clear and sharp experience of the spirit is envisioned through it. Usually, in the best poems, the two dramas, outer and inner, are nearly evenly balanced. Neither dominates the poem. The poem can be read with equal interest at either level, but it is experienced, ideally, at both.

A lifeguard trying to forgive himself for letting a child drown, two brothers striving to oppose the real world with the fantasy world of their tree-house—both are familiar experiences and hence create immediate and intensified human interest, but they become unfamiliar, beautiful, and strange as a unique spiritual experience is filtered through them. The familiar story seems, of necessity, to call up from the inner depths a strangely new spiritual history to explain it. At the same time, the spirit half creates the illusion of being the reflection or mirror image of the story half—the familiar leading, effortlessly, into the unfamiliar, and back again. If the spirit half dominates many of the best early poems, the story half dominates Dickey's best later poems—"Shark's Parlor," "The Sheep Child," "Falling"—in which the poet is bent on exploring novel, rather than ordinary, experience, to stir up strangely new spiritual overtones, and to extend the resources of his art.

In "Tree House" and "The Lifeguard," a familiar experience is turned inside out. As the poems proceed, the focus of the drama shifts from the outer world of story to the inner world of magic. What begins as a tale of two boys playing house in a tree changes into a mystical vision in which the speaker experiences a transmigration of three beings—his own, his dead brother's, and his sleeping brother's—through the medium of the tree. The state of spirits in flux is expertly dramatized by lines that enter the inexplicable thresholds between brother and brother, alive and dead, asleep and awake:

     I stir
Within another's life. Whose life?
Who is dead? Whose presence is living? . . .
Can two bodies make up a third?

The lifeguard returns to the scene of his defeat and recounts his failed attempt to save the drowned child's life in details that suggest the pain of self-mutilation:

And my fingertips turned into stone
From clutching immovable blackness.

His ritual suffering, in memory, summons the dead child's spirit to his aid. Though he is still "thinking of how I may be/ The savior of one/ Who has already died in my care," paradoxically, the relation between saver and saved is reversed through the medium of water as the dead child's spirit rises to free the living, helpless man from his guilt.

Both poems awaken the reader to the unexpected realization that a profound spiritual life lies hidden just below the surface of most routine experiences, and that perhaps this inner life of being is inherent in all experience, waiting to be released by the healthy imagination. This inner life erupts with the intensity of hallucination and pervades our being with the strangeness of the supernatural, yet it is, at all times, available to the normal mind. It is a richer totality of being than we are accustomed to enjoying in our daily lives. It seems to be delivered to the conscious self as from an inexhaustible source. At a moment's notice, it can transform grief into boundless joy. It is a state in which each one's being is both alone in a self-contained peace and indissolubly connected, in love, to other beings, living and dead, as in the beautiful closing lines of "Tree House":

To sing, must I feel the world's light?
My green, graceful bones fill the air
With sleeping birds. Alone, alone
And with them I move gently.
I move at the heart of the world.

Never again in his poems about children does Dickey achieve such a full expression of the way he perceives the strange beauty—the otherness—of children's fantasy-vision as he does in "The Lifeguard" and "Tree House." Yet in neither of these poems do we find purely a child's vision; rather, they offer a vision inaccessible to children, possible only to a man childlike in his freedom from incapacitating rigidities of mind and in his absolute faith in the saving power of imagination. The lifeguard's vision contains, in addition, the belief that a powerful healing forgiveness dwells in the souls of small children: a forgiveness strong enough to balance a man's guilt for taking the place of the brother "dead before I was born," and a healing power soothing enough to close temporarily the wound sustained by his spirit when he poured fire-death on the children of Japan. The evidence of thematic development strongly suggests that the guilt that is partly assuaged through the persona of the lifeguard is only temporarily forestalled, while the poet gradually fortifies his craft to deal with the larger challenge of a direct encounter, in art, with the events of the war which planted in his heart seeds of guilt that can never be entirely purged or expunged. The searing, insurmountable guilt is presented in raw form in many lines and images in "The Firebombing," and, again, in the final passage of "Slave Quarters," in which the southern white father meditates on the face of his choice possession, an illegitimate mulatto son:

        . . . There is no hatred
Like love in the eyes
Of a wholly owned face? When you think of what
It would be like   . what it has been
What it is to look once a day
Into an only
Son's brown, waiting, wholly possessed
Amazing eyes, and not
Acknowledge, but own?

    Dickey's imagination is obsessed with a man's responsibility—human and mystical—for the lives of children, especially those entrusted to his care. It is one of the very few themes that have engaged him deeply at each stage of his development, the problem having its own self-defined limits, peculiarity, and obsessive strangeness. Dickey is always at his best when he tackles a subject that entirely engrosses and excites his imagination, such as the most basic challenges to his manhood—befriending, fathering, husbanding.

    One of Dickey's most sustaining and pervasive faiths is his absolute belief that the human imagination can save us from anything. No human disaster or tragedy is too large for the imagination to encompass or too crushing for imagination to convert it into lifesavingness. This credo reaches its culmination, and its apotheosis, in the poem "Falling." Who would have guessed that a woman's falling to her death from a plane could be converted by Dickey's imagination into a symbol of fantastic affirmation of life? The thought of his being responsible for the death of a child fills Dickey's heart with extreme terror, a terror that arouses an instantaneous sympathy and recognition in most readers. Every parent harbors a secret voice in his soul repeating over and over—consciously or unconsciously—that if harm or injury comes to his child through his neglect, he'll never forgive himself. That *never* is a powerful and terrifying idea, and Dickey's imagination obstinately refuses to submit to never. Some of his best poems, such as "The Lifeguard" and "The Fire-bombing," are desperate attempts to forgive himself, spiritually, for what he recognizes to be humanly unforgivable.

The development of Dickey's treatment of the theme of human/animal relations is central to his art. Moreover, since this theme is unhampered by the overwhelming moral guilt of much of the war poetry and the poems about children, it can be used to demonstrate an evolving logos of being.

Dickey's engagement with the animal world was never cultivated simply as equipment for his poetry. He is intent on exploring the animal's dimensions of being. His experience of hunting, like that of soldiering, antedates his career in poetry by many years. As in the war poetry, the passion he feels for hunted animals is so intense that it enables him to put out of his mind the tradition of nature poetry in English—D. H. Lawrence's excepted—and induce a literary amnesia, allowing him the latitude of imagination necessary to do justice to a series of strangely unique human/animal encounters.

The stages of relationship he depicts closely resemble those of a love affair between man and woman, especially in the way the poet's mind explores possibilities—limits—of relationship in search of a truer sense of identity. Dickey's realization of personal identity is always sought through a deep conjunction with the Other, whether the Other happens to take the form of animals, children, man, or woman. Consider, for example, "The Heaven of Animals":

Here they are. The soft eyes open.
If they have lived in a wood
It is a wood.
If they have lived on plains

It is grass rolling
Under their feet forever.

Having no souls, they have come,
Anyway, beyond their knowing.
Their instincts wholly bloom
And they rise.
The soft eyes open.

To match them, the landscape flowers,
Outdoing, desperately
Outdoing what is required:
The richest wood,
The deepest field.

For some of these,
It could not be the place
It is, without blood.
These hunt, as they have done,
But with claws and teeth grown perfect,

More deadly than they can believe.
They stalk more silently,
And crouch on the limbs of trees,
And their descent
Upon the bright backs of their prey

May take years
In a sovereign floating of joy.
And those that are hunted
Know this as their life,
Their reward: to walk

Under such trees in full knowledge
Of what is in glory above them,
And to feel no fear,
But acceptance, compliance.
Fulfilling themselves without pain

At the cycle's center,
They tremble, they walk
Under the tree,
They fall, they are torn,
They rise, they walk again.

"The Heaven of Animals" is a classically pure statement. It pictures the animals in an utterly unpeopled landscape that recalls D. H. Lawrence's wistful misanthropic vision in *Women in Love* of a world "all grass and a hare standing up." Dickey conceives of the animals as being ideally beautiful and innocent, incapable of evil. All violence, or blood-shed, is performed with "claws and teeth grown perfect." The spilling of blood is a necessary condition of this idyllic state that "could not be the place/ It is, without blood." If the animals' "soft eyes open," they are capable of ferocity, as well as of gentleness, "More deadly than they can believe." But the victims are spared both fear and pain since hunter and hunted alike flourish in a "sovereign floating of joy." "At the cycle's center," killing and being killed comprise a total love-relation, a fulfillment of animal life, since all beings are instantly reincarnated and reborn: "They fall, they are torn,/ They rise, they walk again."

At times, Dickey's unqualified adulation for animals, like his glorifica-tion of the healthy-mindedness of children, verges on absurd romanti-cism. The vision in "The Heaven of Animals," however, as in most of Dickey's poems, works two ways. It suggests that man is the only corrupt animal. If he were removed from earth, beatitude would automatically transpire, just as it must have prevailed before his coming. The vision also anticipates later poems, beginning with "Fog Envelops the Animals," in which man the hunter tries to qualify for reëntry into the animal heaven from which he has been excluded. To do so, he must purify himself, divest himself of all those aspects of humanness that unfit him for animal beatitude. The fog is the medium of purification: "Sound-lessly whiteness is eating/ My visible self alive./ I shall enter this world like the dead." As the visible self is eaten away, the fear and guilt of man the hunter are dissolved. Despite the fact that he kills, he can feel innocent.

In the earlier poems, the action is symbolic ritual; in "Springer Moun-tain," the action is realistic narrative interrupted by the advent of miracle—a plunge into the mystical beyond. If the earlier poems offered symbolic justification of the master-slave relation between hunter and hunted, "Springer Mountain" converts that relation into an erotic encounter between two equal, but qualitatively distinct, beings. The man spontaneously strips off his clothes and runs joyously in the woods with the deer. The hunter expresses his love for the animal-being in a more direct intimacy than ever before. He approaches the deer on a strictly human level, expressing the ardor and laughter of exuberant human affection. In contrast, in "Fog Envelops the Animals," he entered the animal's life-sphere by giving up his human qualities entirely to the transforming symbolic fog. The gains for entry into the foreign element were balanced, or canceled, by losses of realism and human identity. There is a kind of emotional dishonesty in glorifying the animal's otherness and integrity of being while debasing one's own human otherness, as though it can be taken off and put back on with one's clothes. Thus in "Springer Mountain" a deeper honesty is exhibited than in earlier poems. Though the hunter has become farcical in his excessive attempt to assume the identity of the deer-beloved, he has retained his human personality, and even though he ludicrously overshoots his human limitations in trying to identify with the deer, he salvages a sizable reward:

For a few steps deep in the dance
Of what I most am and should be
And can be only once in this life.

The ultimate lesson Dickey brings back from his poems would seem to be wisdom of being. The poems teach him how to be, and we may suppose he learns as much from blundered tries for impossible being as from the successes.

As a poem, "Springer Mountain" is less successful than "The Heaven of Animals," because it is less compact and less technically achieved. As the poem searches for a new experience, a further reach of vision, the rhythms fall into a decadent sing-song and the experience is diffused, not intensified. Also, the laughter in the poem occurs at the extremity, rather than at the center, of its experience. It does not become a controlling point of view, as does the comic spirit in later poems like "Power and Light" and "Encounter in the Cage Country," but the poem winds up a chapter in Dickey's art. Once he has loved a deer with personal intimacy, he can never return to the master-slave relation again. He has hunted "Deer for the first and last time." He is a man who has learned, irrecoverably, that a deep give-and-take exchange is possible between man and animal, an exchange that maintains the identity in separateness of each being. He is now ready to bring to the final and fulfilled meetings of "The Sheep Child" and "Encounter in the Cage Country" a full quotient of human personality.

But first, it remains for the speaker of the poems to stretch beyond human limits in another extreme direction. In "Reincarnation 2," man literally becomes a bird, not merely evolving certain bird-like characteristics as in earlier poems. Kafka has captured the horror of man's turning into an animal in "Metamorphosis"; Dickey evokes the beatitude of man reborn as animal. Gradually, in Dickey's vision, man has qualified for complete entry into animal heaven. In "Reincarnation 2," entry, following elaborate ritual initiation, is irreversible. Man reborn as a bird can never change back into man again, as he can in myths and fairy stories of human/animal interchange. Early in the poem, the man senses that he has been transformed into a bird, and that he must learn to live with it. He still has human feelings and ideas, so they must either become annexed to the new bird-instincts, bird-senses, and bird-spirit, or give place to them. On one level, the man gradually divests himself of all aspects of humanness as he learns his new life, wears his new bird-identity. On another, the entire experience is perceived through the human awareness of the author. So man-spirit and bird-spirit are wedded in the bird's body, much as owl-spirit and blind child's spirit had become wedded in the father's dream song in "The Owl King."

Somehow, the conception of "Reincarnation 2" seems too settled in advance, and the experience seems contrived. In "The Sheep Child," terror and sexual mystery achieve the focus and compression of experience the other poem lacks. Too much of "Reincarnation 2" is diffused in the bloodless void of philosophical abstraction, but one really believes the sheep child's vision because its identity is so palpable, so uniquely realized in language of passionate intensity:

I am here, in my father's house.
I who am half of your world, came deeply
To my mother in the long grass
Of the west pasture, where she stood like moonlight
Listening for foxes. It was something like love
From another world that seized her
From behind, and she gave, not lifting her head

Out of dew, without ever looking, her best
Self to that great need. Turned loose, she dipped her face
Farther into the chill of the earth, and in a sound
Of sobbing   of something stumbling
Away, began, as she must do,
To carry me.

"The Sheep Child" develops in two movements spoken by two separate personae, the narrator and the sheep child, a method that recalls the method of "The Owl King," in which each of three speakers views an experience from a different angle of vision. The sheep child is a vastly better poet than the narrator, exceeding him as the superhuman exceeds the human. The narrator's introductory remarks are delivered with the maundering stammer of a southern yokel spinning a ghostly yarn. In his soliloquy (above), the sheep child maintains that the farm boy regarded his sheep-mate as a thing without being, selfless, defenseless, caught unawares. To couple with the sheep would be a mere extension of the act of masturbation, like coupling "with soft-wooded trees/ With mounds of earth." Shrewdly, the sheep complies with this falsification of her role to trap the boy into completing the act of bestiality. The boy mistakes the female sheep's absorbed passiveness for indifference, for *"she gave, not lifting her head/ Out of dew, without ever looking, her best/ Self to that great need."* The ewe experiences a perfect fulfillment of being; the farm boy, "stumbling away," is sobbing, haunted, driven wildly afraid by the profundity of her experience. His fear is mixed with guilt for having committed the forbidden act.

The ewe takes her place alongside "Crazy Jane" in the gallery of mindless sexual heroines in modern poetry in English. The farm boy's amazement and terror at her unexpected passion dramatize, in an original and unpredictable way, the mystery and depth of female sexuality. Yeats provided religious-erotic motifs that anticipate this poem in "Leda and the Swan" and "The Second Coming." But while Yeats molds the poem around myths taken from Bible, folklore, or literary tradition, Dickey draws on legends concocted by nonliterate, superstitious people to curb the wildness of the young. The poem combines the supernatural otherness of nightmare with Ripleyesque shock effects, but the vision is so powerfully conceived that it escapes sensationalism.

If "The Sheep Child" opens up new possibilities for deepening man's sexual identity, "Encounter in the Cage Country" explores opportunities for deepening his spiritual identity in a worldly setting (in this poem, the zoo). "Encounter" succeeds because the fabulous experience occurs unexpectedly, in a completely mundane context. The astonishing recognition and exchange between the narrator and the leopard unmistakably carries the ring of truth. Mystical events very likely do seem to invade the author's worldly life, leaping into his experience where he least expects to find them. They strike him, and those witnesses who happen to be present and looking on, with crushing reality:

Among the crowd, he found me
Out   and dropped his bloody snack

And came to the perilous edge
Of the cage, where the great bars tremble
Like wire. All Sunday ambling stopped,

The curved cells tightened around
Us all   as we saw he was watching only
Me.

"Encounter" is a celebration of individual uniqueness. As in "Snakebite," the protagonist pictures himself as the *one chosen*, chosen by some mysterious intelligent agent in the universe who

                  was given a life-
mission to say to me hungrily over

And over and over   *your moves are exactly right*
For a few things in this world: we know you
When you come, Green Eyes, Green Eyes.

Most of the poems that employ the theme of human/animal relations try to maintain a balance between emotional extremes of joy and terror. In "The Heaven of Animals" and "Springer Mountain," the terror is felt to be too easily contained, or counterbalanced, by the joy. An irrepressible terror is unleashed in "The Sheep Child." Finally, a truer

20

balance between deepened emotions is achieved in the vision of "Encounter in the Cage Country," in which the comic spirit becomes a center of focus:

> . . . at one brilliant move
>
> I made as though drawing a gun from my hip-
> bone, the bite-sized children broke
> Up   changing their concept of laughter,
>
> But none of this changed his eyes, or changed
> My green glasses. Alert, attentive,
> He waited for what I could give him:
>
> My moves   my throat   my wildest love,
> The eyes behind my eyes.

While the humor enhances the seriousness of the exchange between man and beast, it also balances the terror as the poem rises to a peak of spiritual transcendence.

In the earlier poems, Dickey supposed he could give up his human self to the animal realm. The human/animal encounter in the last poem of the series, "Encounter in the Cage Country," has become a medium through which his human limitations can be transcended, but in going beyond his human condition, he no longer transforms into a new, wholly other being; instead, he intensifies and deepens the human self by adding animal powers to it. He becomes more truly human by realizing and releasing animistic powers recognized to have been inherent in him all along but not available until the fulfilled vision of the later poems. It is a vision which places the living man before us, a man whose daily experience may, at any moment, speak to him in the profound otherworldly language of dreams, a man who is instantly recognized by his spiritual kin among the animal kingdom, a man whose days are lit with wonders that never cease to amaze both himself and witnesses standing by, when they occur: "the crowd/ Quailed from me   I was inside and out/ Of myself."

Laurence Lieberman

About nakedness: understand how butterflies, amazed, pass out
Of their natal silks   how the tight snake takes a deep breath   bursts
Through himself and leaves himself behind   how a man casts finally
Off everything that shields him from another   beholds his loins
5 Shine with his children forever   burn with the very juice
Of resurrection. . . .

(from "May Day Sermon")

THE STRING

Except when he enters my son,
The same age as he at his death,
I cannot bring my brother to myself.
I do not have his memory in my life,
5 Yet he is in my mind and on my hands.
I weave the trivial string upon a light
Dead before I was born.

Mark how the brother must live,
Who comes through the words of my mother.
10 I have been told he lay
In his death-bed singing with fever,
Performing with string on his fingers
Incredible feats of construction
There before he was born.

15 His Jacob's Coffin now
Floats deeply between my fingers.
The strings with my thin bones shake.
My eyes go from me, and down
Through my bound, spread hands
20 To the dead, from the kin of the dead,
Dead before I was born.

The gaze of genius comes back.
The rose-window of Chartres is in it,
And Diogenes' lines upon sand,
25 And the sun through the Brooklyn Bridge,
And, caught in a web, the regard
Of a skeletal, blood-sharing child
Dead before I was born.

I believe in my father and mother
30 Finding no hope in these lines.
Out of grief, I was myself
Conceived, and brought to life
To replace the incredible child
Who built on this string in a fever
35 *Dead before I was born.*

A man, I make the same forms
For my son, that my brother made,
Who learnt them going to Heaven:
The coffin of light, the bridge,
40 The cup and saucer of pure air,
Cradle of Cat, the Foot of a Crow
Dead before I was born.

I raise up the bridge and the tower.
I burn the knit coffin in sunlight
45 For the child who has woven this city:
Who loved, doing this, to die:
Who thought like a spider, and sang,
And completed the maze of my fingers,
Dead before I was born.

THE JEWEL

Forgetting I am alive, the tent comes over me
Like grass, and dangling its light on a thread,
Turning the coffee-urn green
Where the boys upon camp-stools are sitting,
5   *Alone, in late night.*

I see my coffee curving in a cup,
10 A blind, steeled, brimming smile
I hold up alive in my hand.
I smile back a smile I was issued,
    Alone, in late night.

A man doubled strangely in time,
I am waiting to walk with a flashlight

Beam, as a third, weak, drifting leg
To the aircraft standing in darkness,
15 *Alone, in late night.*

Who packs himself into a cockpit
Suspended on clod-hopping wheels,
With the moon held still in the tail-booms,
Has taken his own vow of silence,
20 *Alone, in late night.*

Across from him, someone snaps on
The faceted lights of a cabin.
There, like the meaning of war, he sees
A strong, poor diamond of light,
25 *Alone, in late night,*

And inside it, a man leaning forward
In a helmet, a mask of rubber,
In the balance of a great, stressed jewel
Going through his amazing procedure,
30 *Alone, in late night.*

Truly, do I live? Or shall I die, at last,
Of waiting? Why should the fear grow loud
With the years, of being the first to give in
To the matched, priceless glow of the engines,
35 *Alone, in late night?*

THE PERFORMANCE

The last time I saw Donald Armstrong
He was staggering oddly off into the sun,
Going down, of the Philippine Islands.
I let my shovel fall, and put that hand
5 Above my eyes, and moved some way to one side
That his body might pass through the sun,

108,776

LIBRARY
College of St. Francis
JOLIET, ILL.

And I saw how well he was not
Standing there on his hands,
On his spindle-shanked forearms balanced,
10 Unbalanced, with his big feet looming and waving
In the great, untrustworthy air
He flew in each night, when it darkened.

Dust fanned in scraped puffs from the earth
Between his arms, and blood turned his face inside out,
15 To demonstrate its suppleness
Of veins, as he perfected his role.
Next day, he toppled his head off
On an island beach to the south,

And the enemy's two-handed sword
20 Did not fall from anyone's hands
At that miraculous sight,
As the head rolled over upon
Its wide-eyed face, and fell
Into the inadequate grave

25 He had dug for himself, under pressure.
Yet I put my flat hand to my eyebrows
Months later, to see him again
In the sun, when I learned how he died,
And imagined him, there,
30 Come, judged, before his small captors,

Doing all his lean tricks to amaze them—
The back somersault, the kip-up—
And at last, the stand on his hands,
Perfect, with his feet together,
35 His head down, evenly breathing,
As the sun poured up from the sea

And the headsman broke down
In a blaze of tears, in that light
Of the thin, long human frame
40 Upside down in its own strange joy,
And, if some other one had not told him,
Would have cut off the feet

Instead of the head,
And if Armstrong had not presently risen
45 In kingly, round-shouldered attendance,
And then knelt down in himself
Beside his hacked, glittering grave, having done
All things in this life that he could.

THE LIFEGUARD

In a stable of boats I lie still,
From all sleeping children hidden.
The leap of a fish from its shadow
Makes the whole lake instantly tremble.
5 With my foot on the water, I feel
The moon outside

Take on the utmost of its power.
I rise and go out through the boats.
I set my broad sole upon silver,
10 On the skin of the sky, on the moonlight,
Stepping outward from earth onto water
In quest of the miracle

This village of children believed
That I could perform as I dived
15 For one who had sunk from my sight.
I saw his cropped haircut go under.
I leapt, and my steep body flashed
Once, in the sun.

Dark drew all the light from my eyes.
20 Like a man who explores his death
By the pull of his slow-moving shoulders,
I hung head down in the cold,
Wide-eyed, contained, and alone
Among the weeds,

25 And my fingertips turned into stone
From clutching immovable blackness.
Time after time I leapt upward
Exploding in breath, and fell back
From the change in the children's faces
30 At my defeat.

Beneath them I swam to the boathouse
With only my life in my arms
To wait for the lake to shine back
At the risen moon with such power
35 That my steps on the light of the ripples
Might be sustained.

Beneath me is nothing but brightness
Like the ghost of a snowfield in summer.
As I move toward the center of the lake,
40 Which is also the center of the moon,
I am thinking of how I may be
The savior of one

Who has already died in my care.
The dark trees fade from around me.
45 The moon's dust hovers together.
I call softly out, and the child's
Voice answers through blinding water.
Patiently, slowly,

He rises, dilating to break
50 The surface of stone with his forehead.

He is one I do not remember
Having ever seen in his life.
The ground I stand on is trembling
Upon his smile.

55 I wash the black mud from my hands.
On a light given off by the grave
I kneel in the quick of the moon
At the heart of a distant forest
And hold in my arms a child
60 Of water, water, water.

IN THE TREE HOUSE AT NIGHT

And now the green household is dark.
The half-moon completely is shining
On the earth-lighted tops of the trees.
To be dead, a house must be still.
5 The floor and the walls wave me slowly;
I am deep in them over my head.
The needles and pine cones about me

Are full of small birds at their roundest,
Their fists without mercy gripping
10 Hard down through the tree to the roots
To sing back at light when they feel it.
We lie here like angels in bodies,
My brothers and I, one dead,
The other asleep from much living,

15 In mid-air huddled beside me.
Dark climbed to us here as we climbed
Up the nails I have hammered all day
Through the sprained, comic rungs of the ladder
Of broom handles, crate slats, and laths
20 Foot by foot up the trunk to the branches
Where we came out at last over lakes

Of leaves, of fields disencumbered of earth
That move with the moves of the spirit.
Each nail that sustains us I set here;
25 Each nail in the house is now steadied
By my dead brother's huge, freckled hand.
Through the years, he has pointed his hammer
Up into these limbs, and told us

That we must ascend, and all lie here.
30 Step after step he has brought me,
Embracing the trunk as his body,
Shaking its limbs with my heartbeat,
Till the pine cones danced without wind
And fell from the branches like apples.
35 In the arm-slender forks of our dwelling

I breathe my live brother's light hair.
The blanket around us becomes
As solid as stone, and it sways.
With all my heart, I close
40 The blue, timeless eye of my mind.
Wind springs, as my dead brother smiles
And touches the tree at the root;

A shudder of joy runs up
The trunk; the needles tingle;
45 One bird uncontrollably cries.
The wind changes round, and I stir
Within another's life. Whose life?
Who is dead? Whose presence is living?
When may I fall strangely to earth,

50 Who am nailed to this branch by a spirit?
Can two bodies make up a third?
To sing, must I feel the world's light?
My green, graceful bones fill the air
With sleeping birds. Alone, alone
55 And with them I move gently.
I move at the heart of the world.

THE HOSPITAL WINDOW

I have just come down from my father.
Higher and higher he lies
Above me in a blue light
Shed by a tinted window.
5 I drop through six white floors
And then step out onto pavement.

Still feeling my father ascend,
I start to cross the firm street,
My shoulder blades shining with all
10 The glass the huge building can raise.
Now I must turn round and face it,
And know his one pane from the others.

Each window possesses the sun
As though it burned there on a wick.
15 I wave, like a man catching fire.
All the deep-dyed windowpanes flash,
And, behind them, all the white rooms
They turn to the color of Heaven.

Ceremoniously, gravely, and weakly,
20 Dozens of pale hands are waving
Back, from inside their flames.
Yet one pure pane among these
Is the bright, erased blankness of nothing.
I know that my father is there,

25 In the shape of his death still living.
The traffic increases around me
Like a madness called down on my head.
The horns blast at me like shotguns,
And drivers lean out, driven crazy—
30 But now my propped-up father

Lifts his arm out of stillness at last.
The light from the window strikes me
And I turn as blue as a soul,

As the moment when I was born.
35 I am not afraid for my father—
Look! He is grinning; he is not

Afraid for my life, either,
As the wild engines stand at my knees
Shredding their gears and roaring,
40 And I hold each car in its place
For miles, inciting its horn
To blow down the walls of the world

That the dying may float without fear
In the bold blue gaze of my father.
45 Slowly I move to the sidewalk
With my pin-tingling hand half dead
At the end of my bloodless arm.
I carry it off in amazement,

High, still higher, still waving,
50 My recognized face fully mortal,
Yet not; not at all, in the pale,
Drained, otherworldly, stricken,
Created hue of stained glass.
I have just come down from my father.

THE DUSK OF HORSES

Right under their noses, the green
Of the field is paling away
Because of something fallen from the sky.

They see this, and put down
5 Their long heads deeper in grass
That only just escapes reflecting them

As the dream of a millpond would.
The color green flees over the grass
Like an insect, following the red sun over

10 The next hill. The grass is white.
There is no cloud so dark and white at once;
There is no pool at dawn that deepens

Their faces and thirsts as this does.
Now they are feeding on solid
15 Cloud, and, one by one,

With nails as silent as stars among the wood
Hewed down years ago and now rotten,
The stalls are put up around them.

Now if they lean, they come
20 On wood on any side. Not touching it, they sleep.
No beast ever lived who understood

What happened among the sun's fields,
Or cared why the color of grass
Fled over the hill while he stumbled,

25 Led by the halter to sleep
On his four taxed, worthy legs.
Each thinks he awakens where

The sun is black on the rooftop,
That the green is dancing in the next pasture,
30 And that the way to sleep

In a cloud, or in a risen lake,
Is to walk as though he were still
In the drained field standing, head down,

To pretend to sleep when led,
35 And thus to go under the ancient white
Of the meadow, as green goes

And whiteness comes up through his face
Holding stars and rotten rafters,
Quiet, fragrant, and relieved.

SPRINGER MOUNTAIN

Four sweaters are woven upon me,
All black, all sweating and waiting,
And a sheepherder's coat's wool hood,
Buttoned strainingly, holds my eyes
5 With their sight deepfrozen outside them
From their gaze toward a single tree.
I am here where I never have been,
In the limbs of my warmest clothes,
Waiting for light to crawl, weakly
10 From leaf to dead leaf onto leaf
Down the western side of the mountain.
Deer sleeping in light far above me

Have already woken, and moved,
In step with the sun moving strangely
15 Down toward the dark knit of my thicket
Where my breath takes shape on the air
Like a white helmet come from the lungs.
The one tree I hope for goes inward
And reaches the limbs of its gold.

20 My eyesight hangs partly between
   Two twigs on the upslanting ground,
   Then steps like a god from the dead
   Wet of a half-rotted oak log
   Steeply into the full of my brow.
25 My thighbones groaningly break

   Upward, releasing my body
   To climb, and to find among humus
   New insteps made of snapped sticks.
   On my back the faggot of arrows
30 Rattles and scratches its feathers.

   I go up over logs slowly
   On my painfully reborn legs,
   My ears putting out vast hearing
   Among the invisible animals,
35 Passing under thin branches held still,
   Kept formed all night as they were
   By the thought of predictable light.
   The sun comes openly in
   To my mouth, and is blown out white,

40 But no deer is anywhere near me.
   I sit down and wait as in darkness.

   The sweat goes dead at the roots

   Of my hair: a deer is created
   Descending, then standing and looking.
45 The sun stands and waits for his horns

   To move. I may be there, also,
   Between them, in head bones uplifted
   Like a man in an animal tree
   Nailed until light comes:
50 A dream of the unfeared hunter
   Who has formed in his brain in the dark
   And rose with light into his horns,
   Naked, and I have turned younger

At forty than I ever have been.
55 I hang my longbow on a branch.
The buck leaps away and then stops,
And I step forward, stepping out

Of my shadow and pulling over
My head one dark heavy sweater
60 After another, my dungarees falling
Till they can be kicked away,
Boots, socks, all that is on me
Off. The world catches fire.
I put an unbearable light
65 Into breath skinned alive of its garments:
I think, beginning with laurel,

Like a beast loving
With the whole god bone of his horns:
The green of excess is upon me
70 Like deer in fir thickets in winter
Stamping and dreaming of men
Who will kneel with them naked to break
The ice from streams with their faces
And drink from the lifespring of beasts.
75 He is moving. I am with him

Down the shuddering hillside moving
Through trees and around, inside
And out of stumps and groves
Of laurel and slash pine,
80 Through hip-searing branches and thorn
Brakes, unprotected and sure,
Winding down to the waters of life
Where they stand petrified in a creek bed
Yet melt and flow from the hills
85 At the touch of an animal visage,

Rejoicing wherever I come to
With the gold of my breast unwrapped,
My crazed laughter pure as good church-cloth,
My brain dazed and pointed with trying
90 To grow horns, glad that it cannot,
For a few steps deep in the dance
Of what I most am and should be
And can be only once in this life.
He is gone below, and I limp
95 To look for my clothes in the world,

A middle-aged, softening man
Grinning and shaking his head
In amazement to last him forever.
I put on the warm-bodied wool,
100 The four sweaters inside out,
The bootlaces dangling and tripping,
Then pick my tense bow off the limb
And turn with the unwinding hooftracks,
In my good, tricked clothes,
105 To hunt, under Springer Mountain,
Deer for the first and last time.

CHERRYLOG ROAD

Off Highway 106
At Cherrylog Road I entered
The '34 Ford without wheels,
Smothered in kudzu,
5 With a seat pulled out to run
Corn whiskey down from the hills,

And then from the other side
Crept into an Essex
With a rumble seat of red leather
10 And then out again, aboard

A blue Chevrolet, releasing
The rust from its other color,

Reared up on three building blocks.
None had the same body heat;
15 I changed with them inward, toward
The weedy heart of the junkyard,
For I knew that Doris Holbrook
Would escape from her father at noon

And would come from the farm
20 To seek parts owned by the sun
Among the abandoned chassis,
Sitting in each in turn
As I did, leaning forward
As in a wild stock-car race

25 In the parking lot of the dead.
Time after time, I climbed in
And out the other side, like
An envoy or movie star
Met at the station by crickets.
30 A radiator cap raised its head,

Become a real toad or a kingsnake
As I neared the hub of the yard,
Passing through many states,
Many lives, to reach
35 Some grandmother's long Pierce-Arrow
Sending platters of blindness forth

From its nickel hubcaps
And spilling its tender upholstery
On sleepy roaches,
40 The glass panel in between

Lady and colored driver
Not all the way broken out,

The back-seat phone
Still on its hook.
45 I got in as though to exclaim,
"Let us go to the orphan asylum,
John; I have some old toys
For children who say their prayers."

I popped with sweat as I thought
50 I heard Doris Holbrook scrape
Like a mouse in the southern-state sun
That was eating the paint in blisters
From a hundred car tops and hoods.
She was tapping like code,

55 Loosening the screws,
Carrying off headlights,
Sparkplugs, bumpers,
Cracked mirrors and gear-knobs,
Getting ready, already,
60 To go back with something to show

Other than her lips' new trembling
I would hold to me soon, soon,
Where I sat in the ripped back seat
Talking over the interphone,
65 Praying for Doris Holbrook
To come from her father's farm

And to get back there
With no trace of me on her face
To be seen by her red-haired father
70 Who would change, in the squalling barn,
Her back's pale skin with a strop,
Then lay for me

In a bootlegger's roasting car
With a string-triggered 12-gauge shotgun

75 To blast the breath from the air.
   Not cut by the jagged windshields,
   Through the acres of wrecks she came
   With a wrench in her hand,

   Through dust where the blacksnake dies
80 Of boredom, and the beetle knows
   The compost has no more life.
   Someone outside would have seen
   The oldest car's door inexplicably
   Close from within:

85 I held her and held her and held her,
   Convoyed at terrific speed
   By the stalled, dreaming traffic around us,
   So the blacksnake, stiff
   With inaction, curved back
90 Into life, and hunted the mouse

   With deadly overexcitement,
   The beetles reclaimed their field
   As we clung, glued together,
   With the hooks of the seat springs
95 Working through to catch us red-handed
   Amidst the gray breathless batting

   That burst from the seat at our backs.
   We left by separate doors
   Into the changed, other bodies
100 Of cars, she down Cherrylog Road
    And I to my motorcycle
    Parked like the soul of the junkyard

    Restored, a bicycle fleshed
    With power, and tore off
105 Up Highway 106, continually
    Drunk on the wind in my mouth,
    Wringing the handlebar for speed,
    Wild to be wreckage forever.

IN THE MARBLE QUARRY

Beginning to dangle beneath
The wind that blows from the undermined wood,
   I feel the great pulley grind,

   The thread I cling to lengthen
5 And let me soaring and spinning down into marble,
   Hooked and weightlessly happy

   Where the squared sun shines
Back equally from all four sides, out of stone
   And years of dazzling labor,

10   To land at last among men
Who cut with power saws a Parian whiteness
   And, chewing slow tobacco,

   Their eyebrows like frost,
Shunt house-sized blocks and lash them to cables
15   And send them heavenward

   Into small-town banks,
Into the columns and statues of government buildings,
   But mostly graves.

   I mount my monument and rise
20 Slowly and spinningly from the white-gloved men
   Toward the hewn sky

   Out of the basement of light,
Sadly, lifted through time's blinding layers
   On perhaps my tombstone

25   In which the original shape
Michelangelo believed was in every rock upon earth
   Is heavily stirring,

   Surprised to be an angel,
To be waked in North Georgia by the ponderous play
30   Of men with ten-ton blocks

But no more surprised than I
To feel sadness fall off as though I myself
    Were rising from stone

    Held by a thread in midair,
35 Badly cut, local-looking, and totally uninspired,
    Not a masterwork

    Or even worth seeing at all
But the spirit of this place just the same,
    Felt here as joy.

THE ICE SKIN

All things that go deep enough
Into rain and cold
Take on, before they break down,
A shining in every part.
5 The necks of slender trees
Reel under it, too much crowned,
Like princes dressing as kings,

And the redwoods let sink their branches
Like arms that try to hold buckets
10 Filling slowly with diamonds

Until a cannon goes off
Somewhere inside the still trunk
And a limb breaks, just before midnight,

Plunging houses into the darkness
15 And hands into cupboards, all seeking
Candles, and finding each other.
There is this skin

Always waiting in cold-enough air.
I have seen aircraft, in war,
20 Squatting on runways,

Dazed with their own enclosed,
Coming-forth, intensified color
As though seen by a child in a poem.
I have felt growing over
25 Me in the heated death rooms
Of uncles, the ice
Skin, that which the dying

Lose, and we others,
In their thawing presence, take on.
30 I have felt the heroic glaze

Also, in hospital waiting
Rooms: that masterly shining
And the slow weight that makes you sit
Like an emperor, fallen, becoming
35 His monument, with the stiff thorns
Of fear upside down on the brow,
An overturned kingdom:

Through the window of ice
I have stared at my son in his cage,
40 Just born, just born.

I touched the frost of my eyebrows
To the cold he turned to
Blindly, but sensing a thing.
Neither glass nor the jagged
45 Helm on my forehead would melt.
My son now stands with his head
At my shoulder. I

Stand, stooping more, but the same,
Not knowing whether
50 I will break before I can feel,

Before I can give up my powers,
Or whether the ice light
In my eyes will ever snap off
Before I die. I am still,
55 And my son, doing what he was taught,
Listening hard for a buried cannon,
Stands also, calm as glass.

BUMS, ON WAKING

Bums, on waking,
Do not always find themselves
In gutters with water running over their legs
And the pillow of the curbstone
5 Turning hard as sleep drains from it.
Mostly, they do not know

But hope for where they shall come to.
The opening of the eye is precious,

And the shape of the body also,
10 Lying as it has fallen,
Disdainfully crumpling earthward
Out of alcohol.
Drunken under their eyelids
Like children sleeping toward Christmas,

15 They wait for the light to shine
    Wherever it may decide.

    Often it brings them staring
    Through glass in the rich part of town,
    Where the forms of humanized wax
20 Are arrested in midstride
    With their heads turned, and dressed
    By force. This is ordinary, and has come

    To be disappointing.
    They expect and hope for

25 Something totally other:
    That while they staggered last night
    For hours, they got clear,
    Somehow, of the city; that they
    Have burst through a hedge, and are lying
30 In a trampled rose garden,

    Pillowed on a bulldog's side,
    A watchdog's, whose breathing

    Is like the earth's, unforced—
    Or that they may, once a year
35 (Any dawn now), awaken
    In church, not on the coffin boards
    Of a back pew, or on furnace-room rags,
    But on the steps of the altar

    Where candles are opening their eyes
40 With all-seeing light

    And the green stained glass of the windows
    Falls on them like sanctified leaves.
    Who else has quite the same
    Commitment to not being sure
45 What he shall behold, come from sleep—
    A child, a policeman, an effigy?

Who else has died and thus risen?
Never knowing how they have got there,

They might just as well have walked
50 On water, through walls, out of graves,
Through potter's fields and through barns,
Through slums where their stony pillows
Refused to harden, because of
Their hope for this morning's first light,

55 With water moving over their legs
More like living cover than it is.

DRINKING FROM A HELMET

I
I climbed out, tired of waiting
For my foxhole to turn in the earth
On its side or its back for a grave,
And got in line
5 Somewhere in the roaring of dust.
Every tree on the island was nowhere,
Blasted away.

II
In the middle of combat, a graveyard
Was advancing after the troops
10 With laths and balls of string;
Grass already tinged it with order.
Between the new graves and the foxholes
A green water-truck stalled out.
I moved up on it, behind
15 The hill that cut off the firing.

46

III

My turn, and I shoved forward
A helmet I picked from the ground,
Not daring to take mine off
Where somebody else may have come
20 Loose from the steel of his head.

IV

Keeping the foxhole doubled
In my body and begging
For water, safety, and air,
I drew water out of the truckside
25 As if dreaming the helmet full.
In my hands, the sun
Came on in a feathery light.

V

In midair, water trimming
To my skinny dog-faced look
30 Showed my life's first all-out beard
Growing wildly, escaping from childhood,
Like the beards of the dead, all now
Underfoot beginning to grow.
Selected ripples wove through it,
35 Knocked loose with a touch from all sides
Of a brain killed early that morning,
Most likely, and now
In its absence holding
My sealed, sunny image from harm,
40 Weighing down my hands,
Shipping at the edges,
Too heavy on one side, then the other.

VI

I drank, with the timing of rust.
A vast military wedding
45 Somewhere advanced one step.

VII

All around, equipment drifting in light,
Men drinking like cattle and bushes,
Cans, leather, canvas and rifles,
Grass pouring down from the sun
50 And up from the ground.
  Grass: and the summer advances
  Invisibly into the tropics.
  Wind, and the summer shivers
  Through many men standing or lying
55 In the GI gardener's hand
  Spreading and turning green
  All over the hill.

VIII

At the middle of water
Bright circles dawned inward and outward
60 Like oak rings surviving the tree
  As its soul, or like
  The concentric gold spirit of time.
  I kept trembling forward through something
  Just born of me.

IX

65 My nearly dead power to pray
  Like an army increased and assembled,
  As when, in a harvest of sparks,
  The helmet leapt from the furnace
  And clamped itself
70 On the heads of a billion men.
  Some words directed to Heaven
  Went through all the strings of the graveyard
  Like a message that someone sneaked in,
  Tapping a telegraph key
75 At dead of night, then running
  For his life.

48

X

I swayed, as if kissed in the brain.
Above the shelled palm-stumps I saw
How the tops of huge trees might be moved
80 In a place in my own country
I never had seen in my life.
In the closed dazzle of my mouth
I fought with a word in the water
To call on the dead to strain
85 Their muscles to get up and go there.
I felt the difference between
Sweat and tears when they rise,
Both trying to melt the brow down.

XI

On even the first day of death
90 The dead cannot rise up,
But their last thought hovers somewhere
For whoever finds it.
My uninjured face floated strangely
In the rings of a bodiless tree.
95 Among them, also, a final
Idea lived, waiting
As in Ariel's limbed, growing jail.

XII

I stood as though I possessed
A cool, trembling man
100 Exactly my size, swallowed whole.
Leather swung at his waist,
Web-cord, buckles, and metal,
Crouching over the dead
Where they waited for all their hands
105 To be connected like grass-roots.

XIII

In the brown half-life of my beard
The hair stood up
Like the awed hair lifting the back
Of a dog that has eaten a swan.

110 Now light like this
   Staring into my face
   Was the first thing around me at birth.
   Be no more killed, it said.

   XIV

   The wind in the grass
115 Moved gently in secret flocks,
   Then spread to be
   Nothing, just where they were.
   In delight's
   Whole shining condition and risk,
120 I could see how my body might come
   To be imagined by something
   That thought of it only for joy.

   XV

   Fresh sweat and unbearable tears
   Drawn up by my feet from the field
125 Between my eyebrows became
   One thing at last,
   And I could cry without hiding.
   The world dissolved into gold;
   I could have stepped up into air.
130 I drank and finished
   Like tasting of Heaven,
   Which is simply of,
   At seventeen years,
   Not dying wherever you are.

   XVI

135 Enough
   Shining, I picked up my carbine and said.
   I threw my old helmet down
   And put the wet one on.
   Warmed water ran over my face.
140 My last thought changed, and I knew
   I inherited one of the dead.

50

XVII

I saw tremendous trees
That would grow on the sun if they could,
Towering. I saw a fence
145 And two boys facing each other,
Quietly talking,
Looking in at the gigantic redwoods,
The rings in the trunks turning slowly
To raise up stupendous green.
150 They went away, one turning
The wheels of a blue bicycle,
The smaller one curled catercornered
In the handlebar basket.

XVIII

I would survive and go there,
155 Stepping off the train in a helmet
That held a man's last thought,
Which showed him his older brother
Showing him trees.
I would ride through all
160 California upon two wheels
Until I came to the white
Dirt road where they had been,
Hoping to meet his blond brother,
And to walk with him into the wood
165 Until we were lost,
Then take off the helmet
And tell him where I had stood,
What poured, what spilled, what swallowed:

XIX

And tell him I was the man.

THE FIREBOMBING

Denke daran, dass nach den grossen Zerstörungen
Jedermann beweisen wird, dass er unshuldig war.—Gunter Eich

Or hast thou an arm like God?—The Book of Job

Homeowners unite.

All families lie together, though some are burned alive.
The others try to feel
For them. Some can, it is often said.

5 Starve and take off

Twenty years in the suburbs, and the palm trees willingly leap
Into the flashlights,
And there is beneath them also
A booted crackling of snailshells and coral sticks.
10 There are cowl flaps and the tilt cross of propellers,
The shovel-marked clouds' far sides against the moon,
The enemy filling up the hills
With ceremonial graves. At my somewhere among these,

Snap, a bulb is tricked on in the cockpit

15 And some technical-minded stranger with my hands
Is sitting in a glass treasure-hole of blue light,
Having potential fire under the undeodorized arms
Of his wings, on thin bomb-shackles,
The "tear-drop-shaped" 300-gallon drop-tanks
20 Filled with napalm and gasoline.

Thinking forward ten minutes
From that, there is also the burst straight out
Of the overcast into the moon; there is now
The moon-metal-shine of propellers, the quarter-
25 moonstone, aimed at the waves,
Stopped on the cumulus.

There is then this re-entry
Into cloud, for the engines to ponder their sound.
In white dark the aircraft shrinks; Japan

30 Dilates around it like a thought.
Coming out, the one who is here is over
Land, passing over the all-night grainfields,
In dark paint over
The woods with one silver side,
35 Rice-water calm at all levels
Of the terraced hill.
                        Enemy rivers and trees
Sliding off me like snakeskin,
Strips of vapor spooled from the wingtips
Going   invisible   passing   over   on
40 Over   bridges   roads for nightwalkers
Sunday night in the enemy's country   absolute
Calm   the moon's face   coming   slowly
About
        the inland sea
Slants   is woven with wire thread
45 Levels out   holds together like a quilt
Off the starboard wing   cloud flickers
At my glassed-off forehead   the moon's now and again
Uninterrupted face going forward
Over the waves in a glide-path
50 Lost into land.

Going: going with it

Combat booze by my side in a cratered canteen,
Bourbon frighteningly mixed
With GI pineapple juice,
55 Dogs trembling under me for hundreds of miles, on many
Islands, sleep-smelling that ungodly mixture
Of napalm and high-octane fuel,
Good bourbon and GI juice.

Rivers circling behind me around
60 Come to the fore, and bring

A town with everyone darkened.
Five thousand people are sleeping off
An all-day American drone.
Twenty years in the suburbs have not shown me
65 Which ones were hit and which not.

Haul on the wheel   racking slowly
The aircraft blackly around
In a dark dream   that   that is
That is like flying inside someone's head

70 Think of this   think of this

I did not think of my house
But think of my house now

Where the lawn mower rests on its laurels
Where the diet exists
75 For my own good   where I try to drop
Twenty years, eating figs in the pantry
Blinded by each and all
Of the eye-catching cans that gladly have caught my wife's eye
Until I cannot say
80 Where the screwdriver is   where the children
Get off the bus   where the new
Scoutmaster lives   where the fly
Hones his front legs   where the hammock folds
Its erotic daydreams   where the Sunday
85 School text for the day has been put   where the fire
Wood is   where the payments
For everything under the sun
Pile peacefully up,

But in this half-paid-for pantry
90 Among the red lids that screw off
With an easy half-twist to the left
And the long drawers crammed with dim spoons,
I still have charge—secret charge—
Of the fire developed to cling
95 To everything: to golf carts and fingernail

Scissors as yet unborn   tennis shoes
Grocery baskets   toy fire engines
New Buicks stalled by the half-moon
Shining at midnight on crossroads   green paint
100 Of jolly garden tools   red Christmas ribbons:

Not atoms, these, but glue inspired
By love of country to burn,
The apotheosis of gelatin.

Behind me having risen the Southern Cross
105 Set up by chaplains in the Ryukyus—
Orion, Scorpio, the immortal silver
Like the myths of king-
insects at swarming time—
One mosquito, dead drunk
110 On altitude, drones on, far under the engines,
And bites between
The oxygen mask and the eye.
The enemy-colored skin of families
Determines to hold its color
115 In sleep, as my hand turns whiter
Than ever, clutching the toggle—
The ship shakes   bucks
Fire hangs   not yet fire
In the air above Beppu
120 For I am fulfilling

An "anti-morale" raid upon it.
All leashes of dogs
Break under the first bomb, around those
In bed, or late in the public baths: around those
125 Who inch forward on their hands
Into medicinal waters.
Their heads come up with a roar
Of Chicago fire:
Come up with the carp pond showing
130 The bathhouse upside down,
Standing stiller to show it more
As I sail artistically over

The resort town followed by farms,
Singing and twisting
135 All the handles in heaven   kicking
The small cattle off their feet
In a red costly blast
Flinging jelly over the walls
As in a chemical war-
140 fare field demonstration.
With fire of mine like a cat

Holding onto another man's walls,
My hat should crawl on my head
In streetcars, thinking of it,
145 The fat on my body should pale.

Gun down
The engines, the eight blades sighing
For the moment when the roofs will connect
Their flames, and make a town burning with all
150 American fire.
                Reflections of houses catch;
Fire shuttles from pond to pond
In every direction, till hundreds flash with one death.
With this in the dark of the mind,
Death will not be what it should;
155 Will not, even now, even when
My exhaled face in the mirror
Of bars, dilates in a cloud like Japan.
The death of children is ponds
Shutter-flashing; responding mirrors; it climbs
160 The terraces of hills
Smaller and smaller, a mote of red dust
At a hundred feet; at a hundred and one it goes out.
That is what should have got in
To my eye

165 And shown the insides of houses, the low tables
Catch fire from the floor mats,
Blaze up in gas around their heads
Like a dream of suddenly growing

Too intense for war. Ah, under one's dark arms
170 Something strange-scented falls—when those on earth
Die, there is not even sound;
One is cool and enthralled in the cockpit,
Turned blue by the power of beauty,
In a pale treasure-hole of soft light
175 Deep in aesthetic contemplation,
Seeing the ponds catch fire
And cast it through ring after ring
Of land: O death in the middle
Of acres of inch-deep water!   Useless

180 Firing   small arms
Speckles   from the river
Bank   one ninety-millimeter
Misses   far down   wrong petals   gone

It is this detachment,
185 The honored aesthetic evil,
The greatest sense of power in one's life,
That must be shed in bars, or by whatever
Means, by starvation
Visions in well-stocked pantries:
190 The moment when the moon sails in between
The tail-booms   the rudders nod   I swing
Over   directly over the heart
The *heart* of the fire. A mosquito burns out on my cheek
With the cold of my face   there are the eyes
195 In blue light   bar light
All masked but them   the moon
Crossing from left to right   in the streams below
Oriental fish form quickly
In the chemical shine,
200 In their eyes one tiny seed
Of deranged, Old Testament light.

Letting go   letting go
The plane rises gently   dark forms
Glide off me   long water   pales
205 In safe zones   a new cry enters
The voice box of chained family dogs

We buck   leap over something
Not there   settle back
Leave it   leave it clinging and crying
210 It consumes them in a hot
Body-flash, old age or menopause
Of children, clings and burns
                          eating through
And when a reed mat catches fire
From me, it explodes through field after field
215 Bearing its sleeper   another

Bomb finds a home
And clings to it like a child. And so

Goodbye to the grassy mountains
To cloud streaming from the night engines
220 Flags   pennons   curved silks
Of air   myself streaming also
My body covered
With flags, the air of flags
Between the engines.
225 Forever I do sleep in that position,
Forever in a turn
For home that breaks out streaming banners
From my wingtips,
Wholly in position to admire.

230 O then I knock it off
And turn for home over the black complex thread worked through
The silver night-sea,
Following the huge, moon-washed steppingstones
Of the Ryukyus south,
235 The nightgrass of mountains billowing softly
In my rising heat.
                       Turn and tread down
The yellow stones of the islands
To where Okinawa burns,
Pure gold, on the radar screen,

240 Beholding, beneath, the actual island form
   In the vast water-silver poured just above solid ground,
   An inch of water extending for thousands of miles
   Above flat ploughland. Say "down," and it is done.

   All this, and I am still hungry,
245 Still twenty years overweight, still unable
   To get down there or see
   What really happened.
                     But it may be that I could not,
   If I tried, say to any
   Who lived there, deep in my flames: say, in cold
250 Grinning sweat, as to another
   Of these homeowners who are always curving
   Near me down the different-grassed street: say
   As though to the neighbor
   I borrowed the hedge-clippers from
255 On the darker-grassed side of the two,
   Come in, my house is yours, come in
   If you can, if you
   Can pass this unfired door. It is that I can imagine
   At the threshold nothing
260 With its ears crackling off
   Like powdery leaves,
   Nothing with children of ashes, nothing not
   Amiable, gentle, well-meaning,
   A little nervous for no
265 Reason   a little worried   a little too loud
   Or too easygoing   nothing I haven't lived with
   For twenty years, still nothing not as
   American as I am, and proud of it.

   Absolution? Sentence? No matter;
270 The thing itself is in that.

THE SHARK'S PARLOR

Memory: I can take my head and strike it on a wall   on Cumberland
    Island
Where the night tide came crawling under the stairs   came up the
    first
Two or three steps   and the cottage stood on poles all night
With the sea sprawled under it   as we dreamed of the great fin circling
5 Under the bedroom floor. In daylight there was my first brassy taste of
    beer
And Payton Ford and I came back from the Glynn County slaughterhouse
With a bucket of entrails and blood. We tied one end of a hawser
To a spindling porch pillar and rowed straight out of the house
Three hundred yards into the vast front yard of windless blue water
10 The rope outslithering its coil   the two-gallon jug stoppered and sealed
With wax   and a ten-foot chain leader   a drop-forged shark hook
    nestling.
We cast our blood on the waters   the land blood easily passing
For sea blood   and we sat in it for a moment with the stain spreading
Out from the boat   sat in a new radiance   in the pond of blood in
    the sea
15 Waiting for fins   waiting to spill our guts also in the glowing water.
We dumped the bucket, and baited the hook with a run-over collie pup.
    The jug
Bobbed, trying to shake off the sun as a dog would shake off the sea.
We rowed to the house   feeling the same water lift the boat a new
    way,
All the time seeing where we lived rise and dip with the oars.
20 We tied up and sat down in rocking chairs, one eye or the other re-
    sponding
To the blue-eye wink of the jug. Payton got us a beer and we sat

All morning sat there with blood on our minds   the red mark out
In the harbor slowly failing us   then   the house groaned   the
    rope
Sprang out of the water   splinters flew   we leapt from our chairs
25 And grabbed the rope   hauled   did nothing   the house coming
    subtly
Apart   all around us   underfoot   boards beginning to sparkle
    like sand

With the glinting of the bright hidden parts of ten-year-old nails
Pulling out   the tarred poles we slept propped-up on   leaning to
         sea
As in land wind   crabs scuttling from under the floor   as we took
         turns about
30 Two more porch pillars   and looked out and saw   something
         a fish-flash
An almighty fin in trouble   a moiling of secret forces   a false start
Of water   a round wave growing: in the whole of Cumberland Sound
         the one ripple.
Payton took off without a word   I could not hold him either

But clung to the rope anyway: it was the whole house bending
35 Its nails that held whatever it was   coming in a little and like a fool
I took up the slack on my wrist. The rope drew gently   jerked   I
         lifted
Clean off the porch and hit the water   the same water it was in
I felt in blue blazing terror at the bottom of the stairs and scrambled
Back up looking desperately into the human house as deeply as I could
40 Stopping my gaze before it went out the wire screen of the back door
Stopped it on the thistled rattan   the rugs I lay on and read
On my mother's sewing basket with next winter's socks spilling from it
The flimsy vacation furniture   a bucktoothed picture of myself.
Payton came back with three men from a filling station   and glanced
         at me
45 Dripping water   inexplicable   then we all grabbed hold like a tug-
         of-war.

We were gaining a little   from us a cry went up   from everywhere
People came running. Behind us the house filled with men and boys.
On the third step from the sea I took my place   looking down the
         rope
Going into the ocean, humming and shaking off drops. A houseful
50 Of people put their backs into it   going up the steps from me
Into the living room   through the kitchen   down the back stairs
Up and over a hill of sand   across a dust road   and onto a raised
         field
Of dunes   we were gaining   the rope in my hands began to be
         wet
With deeper water   all other haulers retreated through the house

55 But Payton and I on the stairs   drawing hand over hand on our blood
   Drawing into existence by the nose   a huge body   becoming
   A hammerhead   rolling in beery shallows   and I began to let up
   But the rope still strained behind me   the town had gone
   Pulling-mad in our house: far away in a field of sand they struggled
60 They had turned their backs on the sea   bent double   some on
                                                               their knees

   The rope over their shoulders like a bag of gold   they strove for the
                                                               ideal

   Esso station across the scorched meadow   with the distant fish coming
                                                               up

   The front stairs   the sagging boards   still coming in   up   tak-
                                                               ing

   Another step   toward the empty house   where the rope stood
                                                               straining

65 By itself through the rooms   in the middle of the air. "Pass the word,"
   Payton said, and I screamed it: "Let up, good God, let up!"   to no
                                                               one there.

   The shark flopped on the porch, grating with salt-sand   driving back
                                                               in

   The nails he had pulled out   coughing chunks of his formless blood.
   The screen door banged and tore off   he scrambled on his tail
                                                               slid

70 Curved   did a thing from another world   and was out of his ele-
                                                               ment and in

   Our vacation paradise   cutting all four legs from under the dinner
                                                               table

   With one deep-water move   he unwove the rugs in a moment
                                                               throwing pints

   Of blood over everything we owned   knocked the buck teeth out of
                                                               my picture

   His odd head full of crushed jelly-glass splinters and radio tubes
                                                               thrashing

75 Among the pages of fan magazines   all the movie stars drenched in
                                                               sea-blood.

   Each time we thought he was dead   he struggled back and smashed
   One more thing   in all coming back to die   three or four more
                                                               times after death.

   At last we got him out   log-rolling him   greasing his sandpaper
                                                               skin

With lard to slide him   pulling on his chained lips as the tide came
80 Tumbled him down the steps as the first night wave went under the floor.
He drifted off   head back   belly white as the moon. What could
                                                    I do but buy
That house   for the one black mark still there   against death   a
                                                    forehead-
toucher in the room he circles beneath   and has been invited to
                                                    wreck?
Blood hard as iron on the wall   black with time   still bloodlike
85 Can be touched whenever the brow is drunk enough: all changes:
                                                    Memory:
Something like three-dimensional dancing in the limbs   with age
Feeling more in two worlds than one   in all worlds the growing en-
                                                    counters.

PURSUIT FROM UNDER

Often, in these blue meadows,
I hear what passes for the bark of seals

And on August week ends the cold of a personal ice age
Comes up through my bare feet
5 Which are trying to walk like a boy's again
So that nothing on earth can have changed
On the ground where I was raised.

The dark grass here is like
The pads of mukluks going on and on

10 Because I once burned kerosene to read
Myself near the North Pole
In the journal of Artic explorers
Found, years after death, preserved
In a tent, part of whose canvas they had eaten

15 Before the last entry.
All over my father's land

The seal holes sigh like an organ,
And one entry carries more terror
Than the blank page that signified death
20 In 1912, on the icecap.
It says that, under the ice,

The killer whale darts and distorts,
Cut down by the flawing glass

To a weasel's shadow,
25 And when, through his ceiling, he sees
Anything darker than snow
He falls away
To gather more and more force

From the iron depths of cold water,
30 His shadow dwindling

Almost to nothing at all, then charges
Straight up, looms up at the ice and smashes
Into it with his forehead
To splinter the roof, to isolate seal or man
35 On a drifting piece of the floe

Which he can overturn.
If you run, he will follow you

Under the frozen pane,
Turning as you do, zigzagging,
40 And at the most uncertain of your ground
Will shatter through, and lean,
And breathe frankly in your face

An enormous breath smelling of fish.
With the stale lungs staining your air

45 You know the unsaid recognition
Of which the explorers died:
They had been given an image
Of how the downed dead pursue us.
They knew, as they starved to death,

50 That not only in the snow
But in the family field

The small shadow moves,
And under bare feet in the summer:
That somewhere the turf will heave,
55 And the outraged breath of the dead,
So long held, will form

Unbreathably around the living.
The cows low oddly here

As I pass, a small bidden shape
60 Going with me, trembling like foxfire
Under my heels and their hooves.
I shall write this by kerosene,
Pitch a tent in the pasture, and starve.

THE FIEND

He has only to pass by a tree   moodily walking   head down
A worried accountant   not with it   and he is swarming
He is gliding up the underside light of leaves   upfloating
In a seersucker suit   passing window after window of her building.
5 He finds her at last, chewing gum   talking on the telephone.
The wind sways him softly   comfortably sighing   she must bathe
Or sleep.   She gets up, and he follows her along the branch
Into another room.   She stands there for a moment   and the teddy
                                                                        bear
On the bed feels its guts spin as she takes it by the leg and tosses
10 It off.   She touches one button at her throat, and rigor mortis
Slithers into his pockets, making everything there—keys, pen
and secret love—stand up.   He brings from those depths the knife
And flicks it open   it glints on the moon one time   carries
Through the dead walls   making a wormy static on the TV screen.
15 He parts the swarm of gnats that live excitedly at this perilous level

Parts the rarefied light high windows give out into inhabited trees
Opens his lower body to the moon.   This night the apartments are
sinking

To ground level   burying their sleepers in the soil   burying all floors
But the one where a sullen shopgirl gets ready to take a shower,
20 Her hair in rigid curlers, and the rest.   When she gives up
Her aqua terry-cloth robe the wind quits in mid-tree   the birds
Freeze to their perches round his head   a purely human light
Comes out of a one-man oak   around her an energy field   she
stands

Rooted   not turning to anything else   then begins to move like a
saint
25 Her stressed nipples rising like things about to crawl off her   as he
gets

A hold on himself. With that clasp she changes   senses   something

Some breath through the fragile walls   some all-seeing eye
Of God   some touch that enfolds her body   some hand come up
out of roots
That carries her as she moves   swaying   at this rare height. She
wraps

30 The curtain around her and streams. The room fades. Then coming
Forth magnificently   the window blurred from within   she moves in
a cloud

Chamber   the tree in the oak currents sailing   in clear air keeping
pace

With her white breathless closet—he sees her mistily part her lips
As if singing to him, come up from river-fog   almost hears her as if
35 She sang alone in a cloud   its warmed light streaming into his
branches

Out through the gauze glass of the window.   She takes off her bathing cap

The tree with him ascending   himself and the birds all moving
In darkness together   crumbling the bark in their claws.
By this time he holds in his awkward, subtle limbs the limbs

40 Of a hundred understanding trees.   He has learned what a plant is like
When it moves near a human habitation   moving closer the later it is

Unfurling its leaves near bedrooms   still keeping its wilderness life
Twigs covering his body with only one way out   for his eyes into in-
                                                ner light
Of a chosen window   living with them night after night   watching
45 Watching with them at times their favorite TV shows   learning—
Though now and then he hears a faint sound: gunshot, bombing,
Building-fall—how to read lips: the lips of laconic cowboys
Bank robbers   old and young doctors tense-faced   gesturing
                                                savagely
In wards and corridors   like reading the lips of the dead

50 The lips of men interrupting the program at the wrong time
To sell you a good used car on the Night Owl Show   men silently
                                                reporting
The news out the window.   But the living as well, three-dimensioned,
Silent as the small gray dead, must sleep at last   must save their lives
By taking off their clothes. It is his beholding that saves them:
55 God help the dweller in windowless basements   the one obsessed
With drawing curtains this night. At three o'clock in the morning
He descends   a medium-sized shadow   while that one sleeps and
                                                turns
In her high bed in loss   as he goes limb by limb   quietly down
The trunk with one lighted side. Ground upon which he could not explain
60 His presence he walks with toes uncurled from branches, his bird-move-
                                                ments
Dying hard. At the sidewalk he changes   gains weight   a solid
                                                citizen
Once more. At apartments there is less danger from dogs, but he has
For those a super-quiet hand   a hand to calm sparrows and rivers,
And watchdogs in half-tended bushes lie with him watching their women
65 Undress   the dog's honest eyes and the man's the same pure beast's
Comprehending the same essentials. Not one of these beheld would ever
                                                give
Him a second look   but he gives them all a first look that goes
On and on   conferring immortality while it lasts   while the sub-
                                                urb's leaves
Hold still enough   while whatever dog he has with him holds its
                                                breath
70 Yet seems to thick-pant   impatient as he with the indifferent men

Drifting in and out of the rooms   or staying on, too tired to move
Reading the sports page   dozing   plainly unworthy   for what
                                                          women want
Dwells in bushes and trees: what they want is to look outward,

To look with the light streaming into the April limbs   to stand
                                                          straighter
75 While their husbands' lips dry out   feeling that something is there
That could dwell in no earthly house: that in poplar trees or beneath
The warped roundabout of the clothesline   in the sordid disorder
Of communal backyards   some being is there in the shrubs
Sitting comfortably on a child's striped rubber ball filled with rainwater
80 Muffling his glasses with a small studious hand against a sudden
Flash of houselight from within   or flash from himself   a needle's
                                                          eye
Uncontrollable   blaze of uncompromised being. Ah, the lingerie
Hung in the bathroom! The domestic motions of single girls living to-
                                                          gether
A plump girl girding her loins against her moon-summoned blood:
85 In that moon he stands   the only male lit by it, covered with leaf-
                                                          shapes.
He coughs, and the smallest root responds   and in his lust he is set
By the wind in motion. That movement can restore the green eyes
Of middle age   looking   renewed   through the qualified light
Not quite reaching him where he stands again on the usual branch
90 Of his oldest love   his tie not loosened   a plastic shield
In his breast pocket full of pencils and ballpoint pens given him by sales-
                                                          men
His hat correctly placed to shade his eyes   a natural gambler's tilt
And in summer wears an eyeshade   a straw hat Caribbean style.
In some guise or other he is near them when they are weeping without
                                                          sound
95 When the teen-age son has quit school   when the girl has broken up
With the basketball star   when the banker walks out on his wife.
He sees mothers counsel desperately with pulsing girls face down
On beds full of overstuffed beasts   sees men dress as women
In ante-bellum costumes with bonnets   sees doctors come, looking
                                                          oddly
100 Like himself   though inside the houses   worming a medical arm

Up under the cringing covers   sees children put angrily to bed
Sees one told an invisible fairy story   with lips moving silently as his
Are also moving   the book's few pages bright. It will take years
But at last he will shed his leaves   burn his roots   give up
105 Invisibility   will step out   will make himself known to the one
He cannot see loosen her blouse   take off luxuriously   with lips
Compressed against her mouth-stain   her dress   her stockings
Her magic underwear.   To that one he will come   up frustrated pines
Down alleys   through window blinds   blind windows   kitchen
doors
110 On summer evenings. It will be something small that sets him off:
Perhaps a pair of lace pants on a clothesline   gradually losing
Water to the sun   filling out in the warm light with a well-rounded
Feminine wind as he watches   having spent so many sleepless nights
Because of her   because of her hand on a shade always coming
down
115 In his face   not leaving even a shadow stripped naked upon the
brown paper
Waiting for her now in a green outdated car with a final declaration
Of love   pretending to read   and when she comes and takes down
Her pants, he will casually follow her in   like a door-to-door sales-
man
The godlike movement of trees stiffening with him   the light
120 Of a hundred favored windows   gone wrong somewhere in his
glasses
Where his knocked-off panama hat was   in his painfully vanishing
hair.

THE SHEEP CHILD

Farm boys wild to couple
With anything   with soft-wooded trees
With mounds of earth   mounds
Of pinestraw   will keep themselves off
5 Animals by legends of their own:
In the hay-tunnel dark
And dung of barns, they will
Say   I have heard tell

That in a museum in Atlanta
10 Way back in a corner somewhere
There's this thing that's only half
Sheep   like a woolly baby
Pickled in alcohol   because
Those things can't live   his eyes
15 Are open   but you can't stand to look
I heard from somebody who . . .

But this is now almost all
Gone. The boys have taken
Their own true wives in the city,
20 The sheep are safe in the west hill
Pasture   but we who were born there
Still are not sure. Are we,
Because we remember, remembered
In the terrible dust of museums?

25 Merely with his eyes, the sheep-child may

Be saying   saying

   I am here, in my father's house.
   I who am half of your world, came deeply
   To my mother in the long grass
   30 *Of the west pasture, where she stood like moonlight*
   Listening for foxes. It was something like love
   From another world that seized her
   From behind, and she gave, not lifting her head
   Out of dew, without ever looking, her best
   35 *Self to that great need. Turned loose, she dipped her face*
   Farther into the chill of the earth, and in a sound
   Of sobbing   of something stumbling
   Away, began, as she must do,
   To carry me. I woke, dying,

   40 *In the summer sun of the hillside, with my eyes*
   Far more than human. I saw for a blazing moment
   The great grassy world from both sides,

Man and beast in the round of their need,
And the hill wind stirred in my wool,
45 My hoof and my hand clasped each other,
I ate my one meal
Of milk, and died
Staring. From dark grass I came straight

To my father's house, whose dust
50 Whirls up in the halls for no reason
When no one comes   piling deep in a hellish mild corner,
And, through my immortal waters,
I meet the sun's grains eye
To eye, and they fail at my closet of glass.
55 Dead, I am most surely living
In the minds of farm boys: I am he who drives
Them like wolves from the hound bitch and calf
And from the chaste ewe in the wind.
They go into woods   into bean fields   they go
60 Deep into their known right hands. Dreaming of me,
They groan   they wait   they suffer
Themselves, they marry, they raise their kind.

SUN

O Lord, it was all night
Consuming me   skin crawling tighter than any
Skin of my teeth. Bleary with ointments, dazzling
Through the dark house   man red as iron   glowing
5 Blazing up anew with each bad
Breath from the bellowing curtains

I had held the sun longer
Than it could stay   and in the dark it turned
My face on, infra-red: there were cracks circling
10 My eyes where I had squinted
Up from stone-blind sand, and seen
Eternal fire   coronas   huge

Vertical banners of flame
Leap scrollingly from the sun and tatter
15 To nothing in blue-veined space
On the smoked-crimson glass of my lids.
When the sun fell, I slit my eyeskins
In the dazed ruddy muddle of twilight

And in the mirror saw whiteness
20 Run from my eyes like tears   going upward
And sideways   slanting   as well as falling,
All in straight lines like rays
Shining   and behind me, careful not
To touch without giving me a chance

25 To brace myself   a smeared
Suffering woman came merging her flame-shaken
Body halo with mine   her nose still clownish
With oxides: walked to me sweating
Blood, and turned around. I peeled off
30 Her bathing suit like her skin   her colors

Wincing   she silently biting
Her tongue off   her back crisscrossed with stripes
Where winter had caught her and whipped her.
We stumbled together, and in the double heat
35 The last of my blond hair blazed up,
Burned off me forever   as we dived

For the cool of the bed
In agony even at holding hands   the blisters
On our shoulders shifting   crackling
40 Releasing boiling water on the sheets. *O Lord*
Who can turn out the sun, turn out that neighbor's
One bulb on his badminton court

For we are dying
Of light   searing each other   not able
45 *To stop   to get away   she screaming O Lord*
Apollo or Water, Water   as the moonlight drove

Us down on the tangled grid
Where in the end we lay

Suffering equally   in the sun
50 Backlashed from the moon's brutal stone
And meeting itself where we had stored it up
All afternoon in pain   in the gentlest touch
As we lay, O Lord,
In Hell, in love.

POWER AND LIGHT

. . . only connect . . . —E. M. FORSTER

I may even be
A man, I tell my wife: all day I climb myself
Bowlegged up those damned poles   rooster-heeled in all
Kinds of weather   and what is there when I get
5 Home? Yes, woman trailing ground-oil
Like a snail, home is where I climb down,
And this is the house I pass through on my way

To power and light.
Going into the basement is slow, but the built-on smell of home
10 Beneath home gets better with age   the ground fermenting
And spilling through the barrel-cracks of plaster   the dark
Lying on the floor, ready for use   as I crack
The seal on the bottle   like I tell you it takes
A man to pour whiskey in the dark   and CLOSE THE DOOR between

15 The children and me.
The heads of nails drift deeper through their boards
And disappear. Years in the family dark have made me good
At this   nothing else is so good   pure fires of the Self
Rise crooning in lively blackness   and the silence around them,
20 Like the silence inside a mouth, squirms with colors,
The marvellous worms of the eye float out into the real

World   sunspots
Dancing as though existence were
One huge closed eye   and I feel the wires running
25 Like the life-force along the limed rafters   and all connections
With poles   with the tarred naked belly-buckled black
Trees I hook to my heels   with the shrill phone calls leaping
Long distance   long distances through my hands   all connections

Even the one
30 With my wife, turn good   turn better than good   turn good
Not quite, but in the deep sway of underground   among the roots
That bend like branches   all things connect   and stream
Toward light and speech   tingle   rock like a powerline in wind,
Like a man working, drunk on pine-moves   the sun in the socket
35 Of his shoulder   and on his neck dancing like dice-dots,

And I laugh
Like my own fate watching over me night and day   at home
Underground   or flung up on towers walking
Over mountains   my charged hair standing on end   crossing
40 The sickled, slaughtered alleys of timber
Where the lines loop and crackle on their gallows.
Far under the grass of my grave, I drink like a man

The night before
Resurrection Day. My watch glows with the time to rise
45 And shine. Never think I don't know my profession
Will lift me: why, all over hell the lights burn in your eyes,
People are calling each other   weeping with a hundred thousand
Volts   making deals   pleading   laughing like fate,
Far off, invulnerable   or with the right word pierced

50 To the heart
By wires I held, shooting off their ghostly mouths,
In my gloves. The house spins   I strap crampons to my shoes
To climb the basement stairs, sinking my heels in the tree-
life of the boards. Thorns! Thorns! I am bursting
55 Into the kitchen, into the sad way-station
Of my home, holding a double handful of wires

Spitting like sparklers
On the Fourth of July. Woman, I know the secret of sitting
In light   of eating a limp piece of bread   under
60 The red-veined eyeball of a bulb. It is all in how you are
Grounded. To bread I can see, I say, as it disappears and agrees
With me   the dark is drunk   and I am a man
Who turns on. I am a man.

ENCOUNTER IN THE CAGE COUNTRY

What I was would not work
For them all, for I had not caught
The lion's eye. I was walking down

The cellblock in green glasses   and came
5 At last to the place where someone was hiding
His spots in his black hide.

Unchangeably they were there,
Driven in as by eyes
Like mine, his darkness ablaze

10 In the stinking sun of the beast house.
Among the crowd, he found me
Out   and dropped his bloody snack

And came to the perilous edge
Of the cage, where the great bars tremble
15 Like wire. All Sunday ambling stopped,

The curved cells tightened around
Us all   as we saw he was watching only
Me. I knew the stage was set, and I began

To perform   first saunt'ring   then stalking
20 Back and forth like a sentry   faked
As if to run   and at one brilliant move

I made as though drawing a gun from my hip-
bone, the bite-sized children broke
Up   changing their concept of laughter,

25 But none of this changed his eyes, or changed
My green glasses. Alert, attentive,
He waited for what I could give him:

My moves   my throat   my wildest love,
The eyes behind my eyes. Instead, I left
30 Him, though he followed me right to the end

Of concrete. I wiped my face, and lifted off
My glasses. Light blasted the world of shade
Back under every park bush   the crowd

Quailed from me   I was inside and out
35 Of myself   and something was given a life-
mission to say to me hungrily over

And over and over   *your moves are exactly right*
For a few things in this world: we know you
When you come, Green Eyes, Green Eyes.

FALSE YOUTH: WINTER

II

Through an ice storm in Nashville I took a student home,
Sliding off the road twice or three times; for this
She asked me in. She was a living-in-the-city
Country girl   who on her glazed porch broke off
5 An icicle, and bit through its blank bone: brought me
Into another life   in the shining-skinned clapboard house
Surrounded by a world where creatures could not stand,
Where people broke hip after hip. At the door my feet
Took hold, and at the fire I sat down with her blind
10 Grandmother. All over the double room were things

That would never freeze, but would have taken well
To ice: long tassels hanging from lamps   curtains
Of beads   a shawl on the mantel   all endless things
To touch   untangle   all things intended to be
15 Inexhaustible to hands. She sat there, fondling
What was in reach   staring into the fire with me
Never batting a lid. I talked to her easily   eagerly
Of my childhood   my mother whistling in her heartsick bed
My father grooming his gamecocks. She rocked, fingering
20 The lace on the arm of the chair   changing its pattern
Like a game of chess. Before I left, she turned and raised
Her hands, and asked me to bend down. An icicle stiffened
In my stomach   as she drew on my one lock of hair
Feeling the individual rare strands   not pulling any
25 Out. I closed my eyes as she put her fingertips lightly
On them   and saw, behind sight   something in me   fire
Swirl in a great shape like a fingerprint   like none other
In the history of the earth   looping   holding its wild lines
Of human force. Her forefinger   then her keen nail
30 Went all the way along the deep middle line of my brow
Not guessing but knowing   quivering   deepening
Whatever I showed by it. She said, you must laugh a lot
Or be in the sun, and I began to laugh quietly against
The truth, so she might feel what the line she followed
35 Did then. Her hands fell   and she said to herself, My God,
To have a growing boy. You cannot fool the blind, I knew
As I battled for air   standing   laughing a lot as she
Said I must do   squinting also as in the brightest sun
In Georgia   to make good   to make good the line in my head.
40 She lifted her face like a swimmer; the fire swarmed
On my false, created visage   as she rocked and took up
The tassel of a lamp. Some kind of song may have passed
Between our closed mouths as I headed   into the ice.
My face froze with the vast world of time   in a smile
45 That has never left me since my thirty-eighth year
When I skated like an out-of-shape bear to my Chevrolet
And spun my wheels on glass: that time when age was caught
In a thaw in a ravelling room   when I conceived of my finger
Print as a shape of fire   and of youth as a lifetime search
50 For the blind.

FALLING

A 29-year-old stewardess fell . . . to her death tonight when she was swept through an emergency door that suddenly sprang open . . . The body . . . was found . . . three hours after the accident.
—New York Times

The states when they black out and lie there rolling   when they turn
To something transcontinental   move by   drawing moonlight out
                                                                       of the great
One-sided stone hung off the starboard wingtip   some sleeper next to
An engine is groaning for coffee   and there is faintly coming in
5 Somewhere the vast beast-whistle of space. In the galley with its racks
Of trays   she rummages for a blanket   and moves in her slim
                                                                       tailored
Uniform to pin it over the cry at the top of the door. As though she blew

The door down with a silent blast from her lungs   frozen   she is
                                                                       black
Out finding herself   with the plane nowhere and her body taking by
                                                                       the throat
10 The undying cry of the void   falling   living   beginning to be
                                                                       something
That no one has ever been and lived through   screaming without
                                                                       enough air
Still neat   lipsticked   stockinged   girdled by regulation   her
                                                                       hat
Still on   her arms and legs in no world   and yet spaced also
                                                                       strangely
With utter placid rightness on thin air   taking her time   she holds it
15 In many places   and now, still thousands of feet from her death
                                                                       she seems
To slow   she develops interest   she turns in her maneuverable
                                                                       body

78

To watch it. She is hung high up in the overwhelming middle of
                                                things   in her
Self   in low body-whistling wrapped intensely   in all her dark
                                                dance-weight
Coming down from a marvellous leap   with the delaying, dumfound-
                                                ing ease
20 Of a dream of being drawn   like endless moonlight to the harvest
                                                soil
Of a central state of one's country   with a great gradual warmth
                                                coming
Over her   floating   finding more and more breath in what she has
                                                been using
For breath   as the levels become more human   seeing clouds
                                                placed honestly
Below her left and right   riding slowly toward them   she clasps it
                                                all
25 To her and can hang her hands and feet in it in peculiar ways   and
Her eyes opened wide by wind, can open her mouth as wide   wider
                                                and suck
All the heat from the cornfields   can go down on her back with a
                                                feeling
Of stupendous pillows stacked under her   and can turn   turn as to
                                                someone
In bed   smile, understood in darkness   can go away   slant
                                                slide
30 Off tumbling   into the emblem of a bird with its wings half-spread
Or whirl madly on herself   in endless gymnastics in the growing
                                                warmth
Of wheatfields rising toward the harvest moon.   There is time to live
In superhuman health   seeing mortal unreachable lights far down
                                                seeing
An ultimate highway with one late priceless car probing it   arriving
35 In a square town   and off her starboard arm the glitter of water
                                                catches
The moon by its one shaken side   scaled, roaming silver   My God
                                                it is good
And evil   lying in one after another of all the positions for love
Making   dancing   sleeping   and now cloud wisps at her no
Raincoat   no matter   all small towns brokenly brighter from inside
40 Cloud   she walks over them like rain   bursts out to behold a Grey-
                                                hound

Bus shooting light through its sides   it is the signal to go straight
Down like a glorious diver   then feet first   her skirt stripped
                                                                        beautifully
Up   her face in fear-scented cloths   her legs deliriously bare
                                                                        then
Arms out   she slow-rolls over   steadies out   waits for something
                                                                        great
45 To take control of her   trembles near feathers   planes head-down
The quick movements of bird-necks turning her head   gold eyes
                                                                        the insight-
eyesight of owls blazing into the hencoops   a taste for chicken over-
                                                                        whelming
Her   the long-range vision of hawks enlarging all human lights   of
                                                                        cars
Freight trains   looped bridges   enlarging the moon racing slowly
50 Through all the curves of a river   all the darks of the midwest blazing
From above. A rabbit in a bush turns white   the smothering chickens
Huddle   for over them there is still time for something to live
With the streaming half-idea of a long stoop   a hurtling   a fall
That is controlled   that plummets as it wills   turns gravity
55 Into a new condition, showing its other side like a moon   shining
New Powers   there is still time to live on a breath made of nothing
But the whole night   time for her to remember to arrange her skirt
Like a diagram of a bat   tightly it guides her   she has this flying-
                                                                        skin
Made of garments   and there are also those sky-divers on TV   sail-
                                                                        ing
60 In sunlight   smiling under their goggles   swapping batons back
                                                                        and forth
And He who jumped without a chute and was handed one by a diving
Buddy. She looks for her grinning companion   white teeth   no-
                                                                        where
She is screaming   singing hymns   her thin human wings spread out
From her neat shoulders   the air beast-crooning to her   warbling
65 And she can no longer behold the huge partial form of the world
                                                                        now
She is watching her country lose its evoked master shape   watching it
                                                                        lose
And gain   get back its houses and peoples   watching it bring up
Its local lights   single homes   lamps on barn roofs   if she fell

Into water she might live   like a diver   cleaving   perfect
                                                           plunge

70 Into another   heavy silver   unbreathable   slowing   saving
Element: there is water   there is time to perfect all the fine
Points of diving   feet together   toes pointed   hands shaped
                                                           right
To insert her into water like a needle   to come out healthily dripping
And be handed a Coca-Cola   there they are   there are the waters
75 Of life   the moon packed and coiled in a reservoir   so let me be-
                                                           gin
To plane across the night air of Kansas   opening my eyes superhu-
                                                           manly
Bright   to the dammed moon   opening the natural wings of my
                                                           jacket
By Don Loper   moving like a hunting owl toward the glitter of water
One cannot just fall   just tumble screaming all that time   one must
                                                           use
80 It   she is now through with all   through all   clouds   damp
                                                           hair
Straightened   the last wisp of fog pulled apart on her face like wool
                                                           revealing
New darks   new progressions of headlights along dirt roads   from
                                                           chaos

And night   a gradual warming   a new-made, inevitable world of
                                                           one's own
Country   a great stone of light in its waiting waters   hold   hold
                                                           out
85 For water: who knows when what correct young woman must take up
                                                           her body
And fly   and head for the moon-crazed inner eye of Midwest im-
                                                           prisoned
Water   stored up for her for years   the arms of her jacket slipping
Air up her sleeves to go   all over her? What final things can be said
Of one who starts out sheerly in her body in the high middle of night
90 Air   to track down water like a rabbit where it lies like life itself
Off to the right in Kansas? She goes toward   the blazing-bare lake
Her skirts neat   her hands and face warmed more and more by the
                                                           air

Rising from pastures of beans   and under her   under chenille bed-
                                                                        spreads
The farm girls are feeling the goddess in them struggle and rise
                                                                   brooding
95 On the scratch-shining posts of the bed   dreaming of female signs
Of the moon   male blood like iron   of what is really said by the
                                                                       moon
Of airliners passing over them at dead of midwest midnight   passing
Over brush fires   burning out in silence on little hills   and will wake
To see the woman they should be   struggling on the rooftree to be-
                                                                        come
100 Stars: for her the ground is closer   water is nearer   she passes
It   then banks   turns   her sleeves fluttering differently as she
                                                                        rolls
Out to face the east, where the sun shall come up from wheatfields
                                                                   she must
Do something with water   fly to it   fall in it   drink it   rise
From it   but there is none left upon earth   the clouds have drunk it
                                                                       back
105 The plants have sucked it down   there are standing toward her only
The common fields of death   she comes back from flying to falling
Returns to a powerful cry   the silent scream with which she blew
                                                                      down
The coupled door of the airliner   nearly   nearly losing hold
Of what she has done   remembers   remembers the shape at the
                                                                      heart
110 Of cloud   fashionably swirling   remembers she still has time to die
Beyond explanation. Let her now take off her hat in summer air the con-
                                                                       tour
Of cornfields   and have enough time to kick off her one remaining
Shoe with the toes   of the other foot   to unhook her stockings
With calm fingers, noting how fatally easy it is to undress in midair
115 Near death   when the body will assume without effort any position
Except the one that will sustain it   enable it to rise   live
Not die   nine farms hover close   widen   eight of them sepa-
                                                                rate, leaving
One in the middle   then the fields of that farm do the same   there
                                                                        is no
Way to back off   from her chosen ground   but she sheds the
                                                                     jacket
120 With its silver sad impotent wings   sheds the bat's guiding tailpiece

82

Of her skirt   the lightning-charged clinging of her blouse   the inti-
                                                                          mate
Inner flying-garment of her slip in which she rides like the holy ghost
Of a virgin   sheds the long windsocks of her stockings   absurd
Brassière   then feels the girdle required by regulations squirming
125 Off her: no longer monobuttocked   she feels the girdle flutter
                                                                        shake
In her hand   and float   upward   her clothes rising off her
                                                                      ascending
Into cloud   and fights away from her head the last sharp dangerous
                                                                          shoe
Like a dumb bird   and now will drop in   SOON   now will drop

In like this   the greatest thing that ever came to Kansas   down
                                                                      from all
130 Heights   all levels of American breath   layered in the lungs
                                                                    from the frail
Chill of space to the loam where extinction slumbers in corn tassels
                                                                        thickly
And breathes like rich farmers counting: will come among them after
Her last superhuman act   the last slow careful passing of her hands
All over her unharmed body   desired by every sleeper in his dream:
135 Boys finding for the first time their loins filled with heart's blood
Widowed farmers whose hands float under light covers to find them-
                                                                      selves
Arisen at sunrise   the splendid position of blood unearthly drawn
Toward clouds   all feel something   pass over them as she passes
Her palms over *her* long legs   *her* small breasts   and deeply be-
                                                                      tween
140 Her thighs   her hair shot loose from all pins   streaming in the wind
Of her body   let her come openly   trying at the last second to
                                                                        land
On her back   This is it   THIS
                        All those who find her impressed
In the soft loam   gone down   driven well into the image of her
                                                                        body
The furrows for miles flowing in upon her where she lies very deep
145 In her mortal outline   in the earth as it is in cloud   can tell nothing
But that she is there   inexplicable   unquestionable   and remem-
                                                                        ber

That something broke in them as well   and began to live and die
            more
When they walked for no reason into their fields to where the whole
            earth
Caught her   interrupted her maiden flight   told her how to lie
            she cannot
150 Turn   go away   cannot move   cannot slide off it and assume
            another
Position   no sky-diver with any grin could save her   hold her in his
            arms
Plummet with her   unfold above her his wedding silks   she can no
            longer
Mark the rain with whirling women that take the place of a dead wife
Or the goddess in Norwegian farm girls   or all the back-breaking
            whores
155 Of Wichita. All the known air above her is not giving up quite one
Breath   it is all gone   and yet not dead   not anywhere else
Quite   lying still in the field on her back   sensing the smells
Of incessant growth try to lift her   a little sight left in the corner
Of one eye   fading   seeing something wave   lies believing
160 That she could have made it   at the best part of her brief goddess
State   to water   gone in headfirst   come out smiling   invul-
            nerable
Girl in a bathing-suit ad   but she is lying like a sunbather at the last
Of moonlight   half-buried in her impact on the earth   not far
From a railroad trestle   a water tank   she could see if she could
165 Raise her head from her modest hole   with her clothes beginning
To come down all over Kansas   into bushes   on the dewy sixth
            green
Of a golf course   one shoe   her girdle coming down fantastically
On a clothesline, where it belongs   her blouse on a lightning rod:

Lies in the fields   in *this* field   on her broken back as though on
170 A cloud she cannot drop through   while farmers sleepwalk without
Their women from houses   a walk like falling toward the far waters
Of life   in moonlight   toward the dreamed eternal meaning of
            their farms
Toward the flowering of the harvest in their hands   that tragic cost

Feels herself go   go toward   go outward   breathes at last fully
175 Not   and tries   less   once   tries   tries   AH, GOD—

INDEX OF FIRST LINES AND TITLES

1 2 3 4 5 6 7 8 9 10 11 12 13 14 15 16 17 18 19 20 21 22 23 24 25   SH   74 73 72 71 70 69 68